Making Little Edens

poems from 1980 through 2013

by
Merimée Moffitt

www.abqpress.com

www.abqpress.com
Albuquerque, New Mexico

ISBN 978-0-9966214-7-2

Gratitude

First and foremost, thanks to my kids who have grown up with me; you are my teachers —Amos, Kerry, Lena, and Ursula— this book is for you, and to my daughters-in-law, my most steadfast husband, Randy, and my darling grandchildren: Honor, Parker, Wilbur, and Mahala. This book is for you too.

Thanks to those of my students who have encouraged me to publish.

Special thanks to my sister Gretchen, an ever-steady supporter of my writing.

Also special thanks to the Albuquerque poetry scene. You are family in a wonderful way. Many thanks to Kenneth Gurney for overlooking my tortoise-slow creation, for the poetry salons where we read so many rounds of sounds. Thanks to Bob Reeves for suggesting the title, a line from a little poem which may capture my philosophy concisely, and to Jen and Vanessa for a year's worth of Sunday poems. Thanks to Georgia Santa-Maria, Dee Cohen, Rich Boucher; the women from Beatlick Press; Dale Harris and Carol Lewis, my first publishers in *Central Ave* and the *Rag*. Thanks to Karin for the years together co-editing. Thanks to Jennifer for Dime Stories and all her writerly input, wisdom, and humor. Thanks to Zach and Jessica for rising up out of my class at CNM and into their writing careers making me so proud., and to all my students who made my teaching career so wonderful. Thanks to Rich Vargas, Kenneth Gurney, Billy Brown, and Gary Brower, for publications of my poems in their fabulous venues and reviews. Many thanks to Tony Santiago who was the first to shout out my very first time at the mic a decade ago. Thanks to Don and Hakim and the Traceys for kindness and inclusiveness. Thanks to my mom for good food and my dad for good books. I am grateful to be living in Albuquerque during this time of renaissance and writerly camaraderie.

Acknowledgements

Adobe Walls: "Funnily Enough" "Glass Beach, California" "On
    Solitude" "Sorry I'm White, But It's Too Late Anyway"
American Open Mic II: "Upon the Occasion of Punky Color"
Fixed and Free Anthology: "Nativity"
Harwood Anthology How To: "To Make My Corn Chowder"
Harwood Anthology Looking Back to Place: "Grandma Mimi
    on the Redwood Highway"
Indiana State Federation (contest): "Waking"
Lunarosity: "Burque Ghazal" and "here it comes"
Malpais: "Portland Reminds Me of You" "Snow Dance, Early
    Seventies" "Star Struck," "Delirious," and "Bummed"
Mas Tequila Review: "Georgia came with the pears…"
    "mathophilia" and "Our Guys" "The Seco Bar, 1973" and
    "weighing in" (for Sal)
New Mexico Poetry Review: "Lullaby" and "My 'Burque Come
    From' Poem"
Oasis Journal: "Miki" and "Bossy Bitches, Beautiful Babes"
Pemmican: "The World in a Word," "Open Doors," "phone call
    vote against bombing babies," "Fucked up Ghazal"
Persimmon Tree: "My Boy"
Sage Trail: "What Brief Lights," "My Boy"
Santa Fe Literary Review: "Maypole"
Sin Fronteras: "A Veggie-ghazal"
Sunday Poem, Duke City Fix: "Seco Bar, 1973," "In Whole
    Foods," "Three Bucket Bath," The World in a Word Rant
    Poem" "You Call"
Times They Were A Changing Sept. 2013: "Before the Summer
    Love"
Woman Made Gallery Calendar, Chicago: "La Edad Tercera"

Cover photo by Michael Seth Troxel, 1970, Vallecitos, New Mexico
Back photo by Georgia Santa-Maria, Albuquerque, NM

The 40s and 50s

The 60s and 70s

The 80s and 90s

Millennium

Growing up in the Fifties

I can only speak for myself—swimming in self-doubt as if
    doubt were a
tropical sea and I a bad idea sent off to play over my head
I come from a birth barely feted, smally celebrated with her
knock-offs of Blum's cakes, my mama loved sweet
my father a distant man, to and from work—
but he did that peach ice cream on the back steps—oh delicious
that two-tone blue bike, second hand, for Xmas

she imagined me the barrier to her freedom
if she never held me I wouldn't be demanding
her second-in-a-row, brown-eyed girl
If fed on schedule, attention measured out
I'd learn not to eat much, not to ask for much
later she said she did not know
and I wondered about her childhood
how empty a room she tried to fill with perfection
feeling that being a daughter was a crime

she sent us out to swim in the sea years before lessons
sat far behind her magazine, tiny as her pack of matches
we had to conquer the tide, fight the undertow
just before drowning—my sister and I
bobbing in that shoulder-deep challenge near the pier
hold onto your inner tubes, she'd say, then walk away

she sent me down to the woods alone and to the store at night
running on the sidewalk from boogie men's imagined snake
    arms
grabbing, and bushes I'd get dragged in
is that how I survived—forewarned is forearmed?
she didn't like too much truth; good girls were quiet
the rule of the day

she flirted with my boyfriends and called me slut
hid her affairs and called me liar
she wasn't good, my sister still says
but I liked the clothes she sewed us, *haute couture*
little tweed coats with velvet collars
& in summer's quiet during the babies' naps
we'd order shorts and a plain blouse from a catalog
lots of waiting for life to happen

I liked her breakfasts of Rice Krispies
her dinners with homemade biscuits
blackberry pies redolent of sun
I liked her pretty auburn hair
her changing-over-the-decades eyes
her fingernails and full lips perfect
for Marlboros and dark red lipstick

she could drive like a man
one elbow set on the sill
a cigarette dangling somewhere
did what she had to
hesitant to explore more dangerous choices
her hard-assed mothering
bred a batch of rebels and seekers
some of us of eventually grew
like our long hair, strong voices

Georgia came with the pears in a wooden bushel box

Yakima Valley, Washington—luscious green poster glued to a
box before cells phones, before apple desktops and menstrual
    sponges
before Roe V. Wade, before Civil Rights, before I met you in
    slow time
before we left the Northwest, this box held apples on old jalopy
    flatbeds
wagons in the field, this box was filled by picker families
who worked the harvest, who lived in shacks on the Columbia
roll on roll on, before everyone had a camera a TV and a
    toaster
before air beds, this box shows the heavenly valley
with orchards and fields, curve topped, tucked into rings of
mountains cloud topped like whipped fresh cream
and we, full of peaches, jumped in the river to cool naked
    bodies
where trains roared by before hybrids
before oil riggers moved in like tsunamis
and journalists avoided truth
before climate chaos worried some of us dizzy
before wells went dry all over the West and cowboys
and cowgirls called it quits.

This box on my table is all wood
rough cut, tapped together with steel nails; the pears
made me weary after all the apricots, so I gave them and gave
    them
then chopped and simmered into pear sauce with spices
and put the jars in the freezer for a time after the election
after the awakening of Americans to the need to rise up and
    sing!

Waking (a ghazal)

Buick Chevy Ford we kids asleep, windshield crystalline,
    traveling at night
waking to the rain, our mother missing, wolves baying,
    traveling at night

her red-lipped beauty no substitute for patience, common love,
    auburn hair
gleaming and sharp, Mother, what habits blinding you,
    traveling at night

slipping out on wet grass, footprints leaving family, I joined the
    caravan
of artists, we slept wrapped in paintings, traveling at night

our plan the moment, rare respites in ocean lofts, Victorian
    garrets
desert beds, reveling companions trucking it, traveling at night

renegades losing everything, living wrong, drinking wine
    cheap
in jugs, drugs and velvet gowns, defiant and tumbling,
    traveling at night

riding our thumbs, pennies for gas, smoking down the Coast
across continents, Gypsies seeking an opening, traveling at
    night

enchanting you, Merimee, Psyche's desserts bursting loose:
    seeds, pods
flung wide, footloose sybarites with tambourines, traveling at
    night

Grandma Mimi

On the Redwood Highway
she'd sail us down the coast
a maniac Catholic grandma stealing
us away   her favorite cookies open
up front on fuzzy grey wool upholstery
in her Studebaker coupe
swooping like a clipper ship
in a brisk sea breeze

not enough for us she said
she needed them to stay
awake and I spent hours on my
knees   backseat   hands imploring
(more serious than church)
an intervention a miracle
please God I'm not
meant for an early death I feared
the cookies would fail and
we'd cascade down cliffs
a steep descent into hell   pell mell
and who would miss us all that much

Grandma passed logging trucks never letting
up on the gas   single lanes meant nothing
to this pre-Sesame Street cookie monster
three Sequoias to a load, like us
no sun-burned blackberries on dust-soaked
shoulders, no cafes, no pit stops
she never even slowed so eager to get
home three hundred miles of
curves on that Paul Bunyon of a road
and when we got there, to her drapes and
mahogany bed, we used a little footstool
to climb up; she'd pull back a white chenille
spread and we would sleep the sweet
sleep of Grandma's dark and silent house

Ode to the Booze that Bore Me

Mama's belly tight and tighter in some military shack
she scoured nasty wooden floors
told her pregnancy like a single course meal
her commentary on cleanliness
as if scrubbing could clarify cloudy birth seas
whiskey and Scotch on the rocks
ocean-crashing waters framed her solitude
I was in the way
her knees intent on fixing
whatever dirty deal she'd been dealt

Mama's joy long gone she says she knew
it was the fault of marrying wrong
her booze-calmed heart
spleen, ropes and ropes of veins
medicated to set all straight
like lovely glasses for five o'clock drinks;
oh booze, what a harvest you reap
her auburn hair a tumble Daddy's
fingers must've searched in cold Northwestern beds—
but he couldn't find her melting-into-him
her melting gone to you, booze

Mama rode the straight white track with whiskey her conductor
and I was born whiskey soaked
like a dark fruitcake in rum
never a dream to be but DH Lawrence bum or
Steinbeck wino leaning on a glittering wall

I would see them booze, cradling you
catching rays free of constraint
bottles in brown bags fascinating me
no mother saying sorry to have birthed you
these guys loved my auburn hair thick as seaweed

gleaming like beach-glass bottles

oh, it's easy to love you, dope, then you flip
the coin to blame; you are a power like hate
a fuel melting sand to glass
captured, you are a cold winter opiate—
deadly and sweet, taking what no one wants to give

Mad Women

At three you have a yellow sidewalk bike
you don't fall
the woman down the street gives you
cookies in a linoleum-calm kitchen
your mother brushes your hair
buttons up perfect hand-made cotton dresses
you're at her knees, sister too
little tweed coats, the velvet collars
she puts a doll in your arms
you are photos for Daddy's scrapbook
at three when a brother arrives
they forget about you
not much between three
and thirteen: books
boredom berries & nuns, your
fort a giant Sequoia
Flash Gordon on the new TV
your first diet
you learn you are a reader
build doll houses out of books
try to be thinner for your parents

at thirteen you notice
fixing hair fixes your face
boys are linked to cigarettes and cars
you read Italian novels and Jack Kerouac
confess to the priest after reading *Candide*
you choose Marlboros and every
type of booze you steal for thrills
study Latin and zoology
pretend to eat during the week
three rice Krispies swirled in a dish with a splash of milk
you work silently for your mom
trust it's a plan but they
forget you again drop you at a bus station
wish you well on
a trip to hell different from theirs

8

the babies need your room
someone else will be hired
to sweep and vacuum
your new habits are sex and drugs
being owned by rock n roll men
you only do what yr mother does

at twenty-three married to the wrong guy
loser jobs, getting high, gasping in the sun
a fish yearning to fly

at thirty-three you and your child
step into mainstream
looking for brain food you lose
his little hand in the rapids and falls
you marry the stereotype you battled like a dragon
brandish a two-edged degree
beautiful new babies in *Justicia's* golden plates

at forty-three the moat of his desires
tightens a circle filled with shoes and
food, lessons, soccer
the enemy and joy one two-sided gold coin
you buy your way out one step at a time
a carnival of French horns and violas
gratitude pulses your efforts

fifty-three brings illness disguised as
hazard its tightly-bound gift
unfolding the treasures of every day
you begin to live un-blinded
Liberty's torch and tablet your accessories

and sixty-three, oh sixty-three comes bouncing
a new ball tapping the rhythm
of where you stand: an intersection of lines
infinity mapped on the backs of your hands

Oldest Child

I keep the silver in the high cupboard
safeguarding the stuff of my brilliant father
my funny father, tall face-maker and heavy scholar
who made the coffee table we couldn't put feet on
the sailor with navigation papers who married twice
land-lubbing women, afraid of the sea
one with children, the next with degrees

saying goodbye to him wasn't hard
when he eased my way
mimicking a wise man, his listen and smile
his passions visible as the gardens he created
landlocked but planning escape from his
collection of books and furniture, his final house
a dream not far from shore, rags to riches
buying cheap selling dear, an intentional man
never nudging me toward anything but scholar
I can thank him for that

—the silverware embellished with M
my initial, even the names of my men the middle letter
middle child of the first three sibs
nested by N, pushed along by L
I will hoard then pass them along to whichever child
inclines: engraved, bound by nouveau waves
like the curves of Daddy's horizons, his lust for the sea
and fabulous women, his pride, gleaming
blue as California skies
Daddy with elegant redwood decks
towering pines, his mind busy until his time ran out
Nothing figurative about fathering and him—his presence
visible, the silver a tangible setting he
enjoyed, the finery of a family, abandoned as
detritus from the sea, we scattered, picked up pieces
carried on. I landed with the silver, M for mermaid
in sea-tangled, salty green hair

1959 Sonnet

My grandma was a 6:30 person—
early to mass, early to bed, and deaf.
With Mom and Dad in Mexico! What fun!
The devil's workshop—zip—right to our heads.

Sis calls her friends, they mix us drinks; I'm coy.
I sit; they're sipping scotch and I imbibe,
too young to talk or kiss the older boys
They blab at school about the sweet supplies.

The nuns flip out, expel us both for lines
we've crossed, for rules expunged, for lack of fear
of Hell and God; we're lost, they say—I'm fine
It's public school for us: new clothes, great year.

So if you're young and being bad just ask.
Perhaps your folks will tell about their past.

a common incident

I used to shuffle home
scuffing my saddle shoes along the blocks
and blocks of rough macadam
perversely wearing them out as fast
as possible; allowed only one pair at a time
I wanted yellow flats worse than anything, perhaps the
first thing I ever wanted. My mother's curious
opposition made them mystical, imbued with powers I
could only ascertain by having.
When the weather warmed a few degrees and it was Easter
my mother softened; they matched the new, yellow-plaid skirt
so even she could see, now, the wisdom in the shoes.
I could wear neither the skirt nor the shoes to Catholic school
Our uniforms called for oxfords,
white bucks laced and sturdy or saddle shoes
black and white, polished and buffed.
The yellow flats were somehow sinful, an indulgence, slip-ons
supple enough to show lines in their yellow-dyed skin.
They showed the tops of my bare feet, my bare ankles.
In our backyard, the northern California coastal weather
made concrete walkways a dark grey. The shoes
limned the dark yard at dusk. We didn't have ballet or
     acrobatics or athletics
just baby helping in sad Catholic places. But getting my shoes
     was the first
hint of another world somewhere.
If I paid attention, found whatever it was, I could ask, I could
     get it
like I got the yellow shoes.

Summer of '57, Eureka, California

their color a least-wasteful fruit trick
sun fills wild berries to bust
in yr mouth self-immolated sugar
darker than figs or dates
blackberries juiciest
like someone's main-squeeze woman like
the shiny black widow who eats her lover

blocks from our house I pull the wagon with supplies
old 2 x 12s float across house-sized tangles
of sunny vines near Giant Sequoias
the neighbor's donkey brays each time
our mother sends us to gather bellies' full
to turn obedient fingers purple
resolute with hope for pie or
jam or fulfillment
fill the buckets
she says, I'll make a pie just for you kids

bending behind me at the stoop
handing me a wedge of heaven still warm
I feel I've done something right at last
but too late
her breath on my ear
her auburn hair swaying forward
does she know I love the berries
too much, like that spider who kills
to survive
she must have longed for her own lonely slice
as she rolled dough and babies slept—
summer heating the too-small house—
number five had just arrived
she rarely knew what to do with us
or, for that matter, herself

Nativity

at birth she said "not mine"
you've brought a wrong child
dark eyes, black hair, red skin
changeling foreign but I see
Chief Joseph in each Rorschach
hand-stitching more comfortable
than French seams on Mama's Singer
I beaded moccasins sewed skins
rolled my own, brooms not vacuums
belly laughs not this dull captivity
I can't live in a city much more—but what
upgrade can I muster—the hard life?
that pioneer stuff?
no plan short of medicare likely
x-rays show it's getting late
one heart, one soul, one body
box of ashes
I carry my anger
heavy still as cannon balls
don't mess with me, just don't

weighing in   (for Sal)

My mother was leaning into the sink
elbow deep
Men won't love you if you're fat, she said
I suppose a bomb had dropped somewhere
an earthquake was shaking a village down a mountain
"Men?" I thought; I was nine
Men were big people like my dad,
his friends in suits called me Miss America
in a way I didn't like, looking
from their bird-of-prey perches
News to me that in my future
I would be shunned
My mother suggested I start on It
Get on the scale, she said
I was told to shrink, use up less space
say no to food I loved: candy cake
bread butter jam desserts
I would protect my future by pleasing all
men, not knowing which one might accept
this smaller person I was to be
At nine I lost nine pounds of flesh—
No thanks to Mother, the neighbor boy
who loves me to this day
who shared comic books
cookies and his closet where we read
in little chairs with a little lamp
his Lulus, Little Dots
Archie and Veronicas for me
said Eew? Are you sick?
I got the nine pounds back pretty quick
and Mother didn't seem to notice
As a young woman, many a man said
You're the prettiest fat girl I've ever met

You'd be really beautiful if you lost
just this much weight—they would propose
a number of pounds I ought to drop
Those words by so many I'd never
speak to again: a song by idiots
who would be gone from me like
dust, a breeze moving their
molecules elsewhere
Thank you, wind, for erasing them
The useless weight of them
shrunken up and blown away

I'm sorry I'm white sometimes, or am I just too chicken to be anything else? No offense to pet chickens.
for Virginia Hampton and her White History week.

I woke up white one day. I woke up born white, wrapped tight,
    white, flannel cotton.
Blonde crib, shiny smooth—on white sheets, a plastic holder
    held a white bottled drink.

White walls, white washer, white sink
white steam from Mommy's white washing
white minds in our white house on our white street.
White dad. No one ever said we were white. I didn't know—I
    knew I wasn't Italian.

The swooping mommy-woman, white
applied white diapers, cotton, and white gowns
When she set me free, I followed my white sister
whose hair was soft, light, white-ish brown.

Mommy didn't press us to her soft white breast, bared and
    lovely—not her idea of white
too busy cleaning her big white house too full of white
    Catholic kids.

Who will love me then, white or otherwise, up and down my
    little body?—white or black, pink or golden brown who
    will give me loving
kisses in real life-tones—kisses like raspberries and
    blackberries,
happiness is not colored white.

White lace on the alter boys, white faces in the schools and
    stores
white-faced nuns in very black habits with nasty dispositions

until the possibility of difference splashed like dark tsunamis,
safe as dreams onto our white palettes: a new world
we heard it in Miles and Otis, Dylan and Jellyroll, Baez and
    Davis
Gloria Steinem, MLK and Malcolm X.

We're all one—the pink, brown, the gold and black—
We're all Malcolm X
and I wake up this morning in war time, white, and
think of little green boxing gloves on roosters, so much
less dangerous than razor-sharp spurs, thinking that a white
government hasn't done much right—protecting roosters
more than women who fight next to men
protecting coporations not our nation,
the rich not the working men and women.

Our president now has a chance. Our nation has a chance.
    Every day
I wake up white and I'm willing to stick out my white neck,
    open my
white mouth, and fight. Call your Congress men and women.
    Call yr Senators.
Avoid the void of blank white silence.

Fun for Five Minutes

I guess my grandma thought I could get preggers
just being at the dance, at thirteen—
then again my sister had permission and I
just slipped out the door—
Grandma stomping across the gym but I
hadn't asked, she who was the age I am now
grabbed me under the arm and death-marched me
to her car—grey-haired heavy heeled in sensible shoes
her house dresses blended with mama's wallpaper
that dress would go for some cash these days
all fifties with buttons up the front and tiny belt
and Grandma's passion for God was remarkable:
up at dawn, rush me to the convent, climb the wide
linoleum stairs smelling like steamy cafeteria pre-
dawn food, handrails, murmuring nuns slipping into
chapel with eyes cast down heavy-lidded too early for
them to see a child, willing Lent to end
rosaries dripping from modest fingers
I looked for my teachers
awful ones with the venom of cobras
teeth of hyenas and eye balls bursting from tight wimples
who daily called us hellions and knuckleheads, pulled our ears
beat on us with Catholic impunity
sold us enough candy to fund the dentists' new
homes—Catholic dentists, Irish or Italian—Dagos
Wops and probably Micks—
Grandma came from Kraut land in Wisconsin
quite sure I shouldn't be at that public school dance
where my older sister's boy friends eyed me like a dish
of home made ravioli

mops and mother

I've tried easy squeeze and high tech cotton
but mops remind me of her assigning tasks
I'd rather be walking down the road
or running from tedium or men
or stupid jobs or
cooking and cleaning
Her golf, tennis, a little bridge
she excluded me from everything
I kept running from her words about
snaring a man through his stomach
a fantastical manhunt of her invention
I preferred seeking a place
to be and ok, sure, there'd be a man
but mostly there was me
my mother slapped a bit too hard
kicked under the table called me slut
Where did she get that stuff?
I liked Latin, German, and physiology
never had the right emotions
or body size or dreams for her
never satisfied her mean-faced lust
for me to be her cleaning clone
never cared for clean
or what a man would like or need
he'd have to tell me himself
why believe her, suffering
in tee shirts, rollers, smoking
until drink time.
things to do with sinks and mops?
after divorce she snared
herself a less demanding man
than Daddy. Why? Who's to say.
Her new one didn't mark her bottles

Araminta's Mink

my only mother said
grandma had been afraid
curled small on her bed
neither called nor needed I
wouldn't have had the airfare
my only mother
didn't think my presence
would add to my
grandma's passing
not enough to fly me home
called me after the affair, after
things were packed in boxes
I asked if Grandma had been ok
my mother said no
she was afraid and small
I asked about her old mink
wanting its elegantly wide sweeping
sleeves remembering the side I'd
lean upon in the hard church pew
grandma's arm wrapped 'round me
for stories, too, on her small sofa
my only mother opened the Goodwill box
put the mink in a new box for me
sent it raggedy as she thought it was
the coat didn't have to go to
Goodwill to be pawed on by
poor hippie girls looking
for something wonderful
from a grandmother somewhere
—the coat came, disdainfully
from my mother's hands
directly to me, just ours, passed along
gleaming highlighted brown and soft
a sign of Grandma's proud beauty
I stepped out and saved it like plums
from a fallen tree

Our Father

witty when asked
"What does 'crap' mean, Daddy?"
he said "in the Army when the Sarg says
'crap' all the soldiers drop their pants—"
I saw men in khaki, trousers at feet
dicks a dangling: irony, sweet
sarcasm-yes!!— crap infused
my neophyte mind though mother opined
"Oh, Art" as if language weren't for girls

when presented with a dozen hand-rolled joints by me
for xmas '65 he said smoking pot was like fucking cows
to my siblings' great delight
our mother had a cow and we imagined
Daddy in a grassy field giving it a try

but he wouldn't smoke my weed, or grant that life might
need a lift—his status quo a white man's
dream until the morning we'd all left home
the dawn of his awakening
no wife or kids in his milieu he was free
such was 1970
all his own but we would visit, wifey #2
a tougher package than our mom
the feminist brainiac physicist, his match
in arrogance, she had done it all, the manly stuff
and held his hand until his
dance was done—until he too slipped away in a
last breath at 3am, our Daddy gone
our funny Daddy gone--crap, shit, fuck

Glass Beach, California, 1966 (rhyme royal stanza)

broken bottles tumbled ashore like jewels
you showed me this, the marvel of the day
glass stones, smooth-edged escapees from the pool
marble boulders gold green blue clear your way
no food no picnic planned we couldn't stay
you never thought of simple comforts first
we, wild as mustangs freedom slaked our thirst

1960 Eugene, Oregon

When we moved, we left the warm in California
lived inside a spring in Eugene, clear as vinegar
Oregon foliage crystal green—I stopped eating
to count ribs and ceiling bumps
so unnoticed; Daddy's
cars and credit card meant dragging
the gut so boys
would scream and thump on cars. It rained.
I was lonely assuming my sister felt so too
my room pink, she in the blue, she didn't
speak much, our silent nunnery,
throwing up each morning from anxiety.
They gave her pills I wish they would've given me—
amphetamines might have helped.
Books my only solace, booze and boys the weekend
nights. It always rained
60 days of wet when we first moved, no one
not anyone liked our sunny looks from California
our tans or attitudes organic as abalone shells
authentic as hell and banana slugs.
I could love Fall Creek, a getaway to boulders
and solitude, but Oregonians
well, no, not really. Not when I was seventeen
they were mean and I got meaner

1965

It was a cop who took my trust of men
an offered ride, expired registration
desert floor the stage for his negation
my choices were bullets give in or run
black gabardine a badge headlights his gun
my backseat fear moved to his contrition
he cried I took the lead, made conditions
silence my keys I'd leave we could be done

3 pairs of eyes back at the station knew
4 cops one girl the game was deadly chess
Teresa Joan had nothing on me that blue
skied night when a sinner saw his nakedness
my wife my kids he said; I thought poor fool
his prayer in truth forever to confess

What Silenced You?

Everything depended on thin in 1963
there was no way to be fully me
I was quieted, so Daddy could read at night
sent to my room where
whatever sprang green (as in full
of life) had to stay
no sense in my dictionary or the
pink eyelet spread—no sense
I could barely decipher the syllables
it was frightening just to be, in 1963
being was just, and I mean only, about thin
and smoke and the male gaze of powerful men
a man in my arms had to be ample, fed
everything I couldn't eat
and divine   remember 1965?
you cross-legged on your apartment floor
black-framed glasses all you had on   your
long lean body with a chest that meant business
everything an awfully good fit   sex
like a knee jerk reaction over and over
but I was strangely free   untethered
by your particular gaze   I remember
we ate cake one day like it was OK—
you had no idea how wrong the cake was
me stark naked in daylight holding the plate
licking the fork and the chocolate crumbs
that Oregon summer
scratchy mats for carpets, your bright sheets
crumpled in a sultry-curtained room
of course, you never asked me
never said much at all—no plan was the plan
do you remember enlisting and coming back alive
you, the perennial child, not of flowers but
of hashish and militant confusion?

Dearest Jack Kerouac,

Kerouac u bum, u plain footballer jock
logger-shirted shoulder-broad shameless drunken maniac
guided my feet to greet bare pavement

I stood in amazement so many years
wrapped in arms and miles, adventure on yr dime
so many nights bright snow-shine glory
Hitch-hiking skinny dipping day tripping
u sadhu guru, Ginsberg and Snyder knew too

in manly mother-loving speed-driven harmonious
days of grass-laden hills Marin county blues above sea
be bopping life surprise every day
sparkling u in dreams love-blowing
hot and cold, wild child, Jack, dark flower child reviled

baited by squares, and yeah we laughed, who cares?
yr different path dared to battle narrow minds
kind of footloose rootless daring; you left us, Jack
missed that careening turn to get old in softened jeans
scruffy jackets, adoring women in your pockets helpless

smitten on the point of your words
sweet wounds of your pen
misleading gloriously in the glory days
California Beat-ness, Berkeley and the Mission,
the Haight, Filmore and the Avalon, oh heaven at the Avalon
the street, the big life party
boozing man you boozed til death wrestled u down
and we declared you the winner

Before the Summer of Love

Sometime in '66, desperation foggy and not unfun
sex a sometimes commodity, we
met at the laundromat on Haight
our pads on parallel streets just up the hill
"Wanna come up to the house?"

I'd given him the eye, eyeing
his greasy dark, abundant locks
those electric-blue blue eyes
burly arms, blemished white musician's skin—
his tubby in plain-white-undershirt yearning look

We humped our laundry up the sidewalk
eye to eye
to their communal home
tension on low double low—easy pace
my fate could turn on his or not
—it wasn't pressing

Their drawing room held a bevy of
girls in perfunctory circle
the Oriental rug, their manager
politely passing a joint—
behind me Pigpen retreated
vacating the burgundy-velvet settee
& my aura
he so liking booze and heavy heavy
a teasing, macho man, I demurred

No career moves that summer day—
I went home one block over
to my bass-playing blonde Adonis
who gave me leash, our ethereal tether
long enough for the city

each other's skin and curves
his Nordic jaw and famously sweet lips
always a warm-curving fit
my job not to wander too far
but to keep the spell on him
turn him again and again
in our dizzying search for God

Golden Boy Gets 4-F'd

my parents like lambs
at their cocktail parties
wanted to claim
he'd done the right thing
that he'd gone like a man
no way for him in late 68
but to split for the border
with get-away cash
imaginary kisses
a survival kit but our
Mother cried "Coward"
the word wouldn't buy his gas
pay for hideout food

he, Bowie-like and blonde
got himself weeks of
doped, stoned, F'd up 'n dirty
greasy hair a sign to the fray
go to hell the Army would say
home anywhere away
no addicts allowed no
sissy boys neither not
in this army not in
in this US of A
no body bag for
mom and dad to
say their false
allegiance to their
blank-faced obeisance
to murderous Kings
to whom they would
easily have
sacrificed their son

yet his refusal to kill
strangers
broke our parents across
the sharp-kneed divides
like kindling for the
fire, the certain embers
of self-immolating
and
overreaching
empire

Threads: A Trilogy of True Fabrications

Bodices: Portland, Oregon 1967

I can see your pendulous breasts in my mind's eye, you so careless with buttons and necklines; thirties, forties' dresses from the Goodwill falling open here and there. You never noticed, never a bra or undies to interfere with your smooth body lines, no tight jeans or "look," just loose clothes found wherever and pinned, tied, borrowed, into a blatant combo of smooth planes and round. I don't remember you in shoes. In my memory your feet are bare; your dark brown eyes frank, a friendly smile framed by thick blonde, Norwegian hair.

When we first met, you were wearing an old velvet dress, midnight blue. We recognized each other as kindred; our men played music together. We, their tag-along women. I didn't mind sharing anything with you; gave you a room in my house because you fixed tea, rolled joints, swept our Oriental rug, brought in flowers, walked, talked, shopped, with me. You liked to do everything I did. I sewed dresses for a living, and you took up stitching too.

Remember the time we got pulled over near our shady swimming spot on the Clackamas River? I was barely breathing because I had pot under the driver's seat, no current registration, no driver's license, and you were a runaway, fifteen years old. The cop said I'd forgotten to signal my turn, and I was counting up the years I'd do if he searched the car. Oregon hadn't yet tried the legalized thing, and I knew a guy doing five years for a roach. I gambled that charm would be my best ploy (what else did we have?) so charming I was, half-naked in my green and white-striped, homemade, cotton pique bikini bottom, hand made peasant blouse. You stayed back, seated in the beat-up Karmann Ghia convertible, little heap with no starter engine, your loveliness half out of whatever you were wearing. I approached him, maroon crepe swaying with each step, leaned on the fender of his car and schmoozed as well as I could, praying that he wouldn't feel my fear, that our bodies would distract him enough to save our asses. I talked to him about the swimming hole and how you and I always swam there, playing dumb and oh so sorry and yes, we'd register. "Did you grow up swimming here?" I asked him.

There was a pause and then he said, "Yeah, I did. And I'm going to give you a warning this time. Get those items fixed, OK?" I thanked him truly and, waving as I slid down into the driver's seat, he pulled away. We were far too shaken to stay and swim. We scattered the weed as offering to the Goddesses in gratitude. No wonder my son is such a hustler.

But you're dead now, Diane. People said you were still crazy before you died. I miss you and your shelves of blackberry jam and crocks of homemade wine and your gorgeous blonde babies you showed me years after the Karmann Ghia was gone and we both had kids. Remember the marshmallow pie party the day the Dead came to town? Nine pies we made, all like the colors of old cotton. The party was a bit of a bust, but the pies were the colors of faded, flowered aprons.

White Velvet, San Francisco, 1968

One dress that almost got me arrested was rented from Goodwill's costume department in Portland, though never returned. I wore it to a party in San Francisco where I met R. Crumb and was too shy to speak. Marshall and I sat at a table sipping tea and smoking with him, but celebrities ranked with authorities in those days. The scene with the cops later on was in silent film tradition, too.

Marshall had eaten peyote, and it was a full moon summer's evening. We'd walked up Fell Street along the Panhandle to Gretchen Golden's evening soirée, and heading home, the streets were shiny and splashy with rain. The black and white cop car rolled up beside us as we moved briskly on the wide sidewalk, and I became more aware of the late hour and the empty streets. They cruised along at our pace, close to the curb, giving us a once over. The shotgun pig had his elbow on the windowsill and a look on his snout-face. I was worried they'd frisk Marshall and find something, peyote or pot, but they had no cause to do so really, except for my dress. The pig was checking out my profile in the velvet flapper affair, delightfully risqué but not meant for his salacious attitude. It was, after all, an evening gown made for a jitterbugging, for a socialite from my grandmother's day. It seemed they were considering getting us, and I thought of the girl who had done jail time for a thin blouse with no bra under it. The officer was concerned, he said, that I had on no underwear. "Hey, I don't think you're wearing anything under that dress," he said stupidly. The dress, was made of soft, slinky, rayon velvet; a creamy-white dancer's dress from the twenties when women were just coming out of long skirts, long hair, and high-buttoned necklines. The skirt was cut in flower petal shapes to below-the-knee, six of them, daisy-petals that draped sinuously from a hip-hugging waistband thickly studded with clear rhinestones. The petals, weighted with small, leaden, drapery disks sewn into each tip, were edge stitched and overlapped so no real side seam was possible. A high kick or a swift stride would show, from a side view, leg to the hip, but I wasn't kicking or twirling. The bodice was modest enough and covered belly and breasts, flattening just a bit, right up to a neckline band, also studded in sparkling glass. The bright, wide, strip of rhinestones swung over each shoulder and dropped in a dramatic V to below the waist in back—exposing wing bones and the curve of spine, the very top of my hips. In essence, the dress was backless and revealed to the officers that I had to be braless, a politically radical act in 1968, especially for a full-breasted woman.

Marshall and I knew better than to speak, so we just kept walking politely, smiling, looking puzzled at them as if they couldn't possibly be serious, couldn't really be so concerned with the era or the cut of my clothing. I lengthened my stride in my three-tone blue leather dance shoes—also vintage.

They finally rolled away muttering how I could be arrested for looking like that. I would have told them off if Marshall hadn't been holding. I had to keep my mouth shut, my face a mask of innocence, the sweet and demure shit I'd been raised on. We might've suffered any amount of up-against-the-wall-violence, arrest, even rape. I'd been there, seen it, but it was late and they were tired; tormenting men with my clothes was my war, my fight for freedom. I won that skirmish. Scum bags.

Blue, Blue Batik (Make Love Not War)

Dirk was kind of straight for me, really, but the day he appeared in our courtyard in front of the Fell Street flat, I was electrically attracted. Make Love Not War kicked in like adrenalin to a soldier who smells the enemy. Marshall didn't expect fidelity, but free love or not, humans are territorial. Dirk's tall, blonde, Valley-boy looks and the poignancy of his imminent departure for Nam put urgency into our encounter. There would be no time for niceties, civilities, marriage, love, kids. Our entire relationship had to compress into one night; he was leaving in two days, and I would love him fully, I knew— not for daring to go, but for daring to open up and court me. To have me as maybe his last white woman state-side. Sure, he was a kid on the make, out to get laid, but we two knew there was more to it. We knew he was giving his life, and no girl, no family there, no one to hold him and kiss him and love him unconditionally for his sacrifice. No one but me, and I took my job quite seriously.

I don't remember any awkwardness in entangling: we ate something in the Haight, and then a decision to go from his car to his apartment— just bodies and skin—no bad smells, no darkness. The light-filled room in the morning, a plain room with bare, lemon-colored walls and bright, white sheets on the unmade bed. We said our good-byes. He was a sweet-necked man with California arms. He held me. I liked him.

Weeks later, a package arrived with a brilliant blue batik from Thailand and a letter. I don't remember his words, just the feeling and the fabric. Peacocks in black and blue, gorgeous cloth. He knew I was a seamstress; he'd told me he was a silversmith.

I made a long, straight skirt with the border print at the bottom and an opening up one side to just above the knee; one simple, snap at the waistline. The blouse was straight-lined, too—a scoop-necked shell with spaghetti straps. The design followed the pattern of the fabric, and I used the whole piece with little waste. I wanted to be covered in it. Dirk had held it, bought it, smelled it, sent it to me. I wore it to feel the cotton and him and his hands which had touched me, then the fabric.

What came between was lost and couldn't matter anymore. I wore the outfit many summers until it fell apart and had to be abandoned. Decades later, I went to the wall to find his name, but it wasn't there. He was gorgeous and fine.

To make my corn chowder

first drop out of school for a while
Be beat then hip—are you hip? Hippies were the smart kids in
    class
—question the system we left; you're in it. Learn possessive
apostrophes: your you're yore its it's too two and
there is no "they" who will change you. It's not their job
even to assure your food or safety. You're as safe as you think.
We planted gardens, learned to weave, to live in tipis, barns,
    sheds
domes, wagons, and ghost towns abandoned
to shop thrift stores filled with your great-grandparents'
tools and domestic necessities
to walk away from stuff that burdened us
to sew, bead, pot, paint, macramé, cook from scratch
or nothing for multitudes
to grow things harvest and revere bees
to concoct stone soup in second hand kettles
to ribbon honey on bread to die for cooked
anywhere anyhow on anything with heat
to offer to anyone hungry or just dropping by
We learned mechanics, plumbing, and electric guitars
promoted rock n roll in flashy clothes and sexy hair
we took beatings so you could be free, to grow, to eat
Do all that—then learn why to buy local
Learn how to garden in boxes or fields
all winter long—learn the greenhouse effect
Learn tall bucket gardens and local herbs and roots
find the markets and barter for corn from Moriarity
potatoes from Silver City peppers and chiles from Corrales
onions from Tijeras and more chiles from the valley
grow yr own tomatoes and scallions
grow cucumbers but not for my chowder.
Buy healthy dairy or goat; learn cheescake from
goat. Get a little coconut milk flown from Thailand—don't

try to smoke the corn silk or banana peels;
If you grow weed, I'll tell you
it does hide well between rows of tall abundant corn
Be grateful for olive oil still on shelves—
Write odes to your gallons of olive oil, make love with olive oil
between your legs on your lips and fingers, in your nose.
Butter will be historic without that family cow of yore
Lard will return; use the rich oils pressed from pecans and
    walnuts
The soup: sauté onions, garlic (homegrown), scallions, ditto;
    add
add, add—don't
peel. The skins deliver vitamins and minerals
Stir! Add enough broth and all the husked (shucked) corn
you can fit in the pot, leave room at the top for milk before
serving. Don't boil after milk. Sprinkle in toms and potatoes.
Anything red.
Garnish with cheese and serve hot.
Invite friends. Enjoy.

Southwest Ghazal

I listen for your breathing and footsteps the sound of doors the
    Sandias'
desert air the kids what day brings each morning

doves coo the hour I reacquaint muscles bones my soft flesh I
consider you grappling, our seventh decade doing things of
    morning

the *Journal* shows a woman in a turquoise burqa carrying her
    neighbors' son
his gangly legs in sad shoes his toys tiny dog beyond grieving
    the morning

black tea from Darjeeling steep hills at dawn Indian families
    pick the leaves
I mix with soy from the Coast cream from Colorado easing the
    sting of morning

in elemental blankets we slept under a tree in Jerome, Arizona,
    you forgave me
for being me we drove the vintage Ford to California after
    praying in the morning

you sweep the front room I build up a fire our simple
    employment gold
New Mexico sun mountaintop west to mesas rushing from
    morning

I remember arriving: dirt-lot-depot Taos *blanco* adobe curves a
    haven of
desperado misfits sadhu hippies, Natives saddling up these
    mornings

me bedazzled by women in deerskin-moccasins circle dancing
all-day
their snow prayer starts at dawn run-off takes out bridges
raging through mornings

mud walls veined morning glory blue & hollyhock riot
welcome us
coastal comrades Llano's ruined pools Stagecoach Hot
Springs divine soak in the morning

Pea Harvest Poem

Did I ever know a cowboy?
Did I ever love one?

I only remember that oldie straddling the steps
of his beat-up trailer
playing his fiddle in the bright morning sun
Walla Walla, Washington, 1964

He must've seen us rent the apartment above the bar
the night before, a dollar a day—we'd hitched from NY—
rode the rails 1000 miles to Calgary and hitched some more

to work the harvest   me 17 'n Steve who drove
truck and knew the ropes. I was pure rookie.

From our tiny bedroom I could see the trailer in
the yard below, the long crookedy legs and half-mashed hat
of the cowboy playing
his music sweet and slow boots and belt dusty-colored
real

he knew the notes would rise
up into me
pretty sexy him and his fiddle
the moment lasting forty
years

I never went to talk with him—
too shy of men
but it was nice, him down there
a flight of stairs a window and curtain away

Lullaby

You and I never feasted on halibut or gorgonzola
our fridge more likely to have frozen wild plums
a box of windfall apples maybe some tortillas
and government cheese

I let you keep that salamander in the sink—
guessed he went down the overflow
Later, in the cutting cold winter I recall
I saw his little hand reach up
and back he came into the porcelain bowl
from the depths of God knows where

you had a pond out back of the pasture
a Huck Finn raft to pole about on
no dad, no family but me
you got a little wild but I thought wild
was a highway to knowing life, outside
where beauty mixes with dreams

when I missed you too much
that terrible year I let you go with him
a blue light descended to heal my
worry, to lullaby the child in me
who cried to protect you
I could feel you crying for me
I am sorry

My Boy

Bright snow our nest, trudging to the outhouse
Piñon fires, wooly wet things
Our abundance all we had, the two of us
Then life split open like a nut and you were
My grief beyond reason, the middle season of
Childhood stolen; I am sorry
All I could give and some damn blackbird
Snatched you and brought you back broken
The best he could do
I would comb through evidence
Your truculent nature lit a blind trail
Mountains, ponds, rivers, air
Did I think burning the tablet would remove
Pages lived already, strange rooms, cold cars
No comedy seduces me to forget
This story
It is me, this story, it is
Enough lesson for a life

Snow Dance, Taos Pueblo, Early 70s

Someone came by the tea company where I was helping Jane
in an old store front keep her herb company alive
poked in a head and said, "You're invited; go quick
to the Pueblo, the women are dancing."

It must've been mid-morning but we dropped everything
The skies were overcast, cold pale air above golden dirt
No one at the gate meant nothing public about this dance
We parked and scurried to the sound behind the towering
1000-year-old complex

Clouds hung on Blue Mountain who spread her arms
to the edges of the land but there hadn't been a flake of snow
Already February and I'd been at Stagecoach Hot Springs
sunbathing in January, my white woman body in the bottom-of-
    the-gorge sun

Men were sitting at drums outside the circle—
Every dancing woman had on luminescent doeskin moccasins
soft-as-clouds leggings wrapping up to fancy hems
Each woman in pale skins, beaded, feathered embroidery
winter finery their sign of serious intent

There were few on-lookers like us
awestruck and stepping back to a place of respect
We were allowed to stand silently and watch the prayer: The
    Snow Dance
100 women moving up and down as they switched their palms
up to God and down to Earth, up to the Skies and down to the
    River
reminding God of the way things worked, in case it was an
    oversight
or something She had just misplaced

Dressed in colors of snow 100 women was the rule, until dark
No chores that day, though they traded out as ancients joined in
        and youngsters
Female, only females danced, their moving voice to remind
        God
of Her normal ways of putting drought to rest
as if a naughty, tired child—

after my son

a triumvirate of unknown
gender, let-loose souls
not repentant, no Penitente I
nor Magdalene with hair, oil, tears
no more invoking incarnations
that's for sure, three times sure
celibate, thoughtful, secure

Diana brought the hounds
an arrow-filled quiver, strong arms, a bow
double windows, double door
the sweeping view of Taos Valley
the rainbow a yellow gold pot for us
our backs across the hood the old
blue Dodge slant 6 on mountain desert floor
soaking in the daffodil

later we dance in rain, stack piñon high
link our solitude to divine
I throw stones in front and behind
Hansel's bread crumbs gobbled
by friendly Magpie, cranky Crow
our path appears, rocky, luminescent
a 12-sided dome on a hill, upstairs' bats
owls and stars our companions
caring for you occupies me but you
will grow and leave. I will spend
a lifetime letting go of you and
everything then, the precious time

The Seco Bar, 1973

I remember you, Michael, throwing me across the fender
kind of cowboy style, wandering sadhu
sad man seeking path my face under your mad-as-hell fist
me dumber 'n dirt at 27, you old at 38 sleeping with my skinny
    friend
kissing her in public, god, looking for love by the juke box
in the last rays of afternoon sun all of us in wooden-floor
    nickelodeon light full of gin and desire
Either I died or she did was my snap decision
Alcohol's wild fission of rage and motherhood trumped
discretion when my bar glass thumped her head
a pull on her ponytail, a kick to her ribs
Five guys jumped and you trotted me
bouncer-like to the parking lot
Barb wire and tumble weed bordered Taos Pueblo lands'
mountains and centuries of coyote quiet
I said go ahead, big man, break my face
Looking down eye to eye, you paused
What stopped you, I wonder
Some mercy for me, orphan boy; did you see me?
The crazy want for you, my same want to be done with you
your hand proved more hopeful than hate.
In that Arroyo Seco showdown, I saved face twice
not knowing I'd leave you behind anyway—
the lone subtracted factor
both of us wanting a mother's arms
the triangular strength of family elusive until
we grew, each into our own
I didn't know yet of two more babies who would
play French horn and viola with confidence
who would never guess I pulled my voice out of
my boot one night and knocked a woman upside her head
that one lump on her sorry, split-tongue face opened me like
a town of possibilities
Before anyone could depend on me for nada
I had to be my own ass-kicking best friend first

Maypole

While they lined up for gas in '72
I pushed you in a vintage buggy
our only wheels—no man, no car
we meandered our way
recession inconsequential to a welfare mom
steeped in categories like poor and single
serene as tiny daisies in the grass I
had nothing to squander
sewing dresses and skirts
selling at the Saturday market
living on so little
yet I returned
I the pretty maiden
holding you like a ribbon
dancing round and round
waving feathers
as if I needed your father to
burn us alive

1963 for Kathy

I got mostly straight A's—straight
even though I kissed you on the lips in the hall
by your locker and rumors had it
we were lovers suspected by those
with free minds—my mind did not go there

I loved your shiny hair but mostly shiny self
of bounce and smile, how you walked
the city and taught me guitar and song and that
upstairs blues club. Before you, I lost
everyone with every move
I wanted you to need me and I kissed you
glad to see you like 12-steppers
helping by being there; I loved your room
with the window, your grassy yard and willow tree

then I had to go, cast out from family
you and I, we loved, if
we loved at all, the same blue-eyed boy/man
in stupid teen-age booze-crazed flaming passion so
you never trusted, never let me kiss
your sweet face again, both of us awakened
to the catastrophe of loss, losing you more painful than
blood kin who closed my own door on me—
I found lips on lovers who would care for me
I found my way, years and years of path and seek
surviving as we do, but I still miss you

Absolute

A for each of us—hard won
Babies kept: you, you, and you, bedeviled task to divinity
Oh, Brother, can you be a baby's daddy, can you?
Rare, unfinished, preempted, I let you pass reluctantly
Two men were one too many, one was not enough
I made a cool breeze pact and kept our Goddess' words
Ovaries intact until that last drop of joyous blood
Now sweet reaping of grandma's men-o-pausal bliss

Divine Fit Sewing

my business was to feed us, get gas in the old slant-6
get piñon, a little cedar, mill ends in the wood pile
high up on Witch's Mountain, the dome, 12-sided
two stories, running water in the bathroom
our kitchen a table, an oven, an air-tight Ashley the
landlord's delight. Handsome as he
was and pedigreed, he asked a time or two
pounded on my door and grabbed
my arm the night of the Persieds
or Haley's comet
I stepped outside to see
stars weeping down as if willows
yes, a lone Taos night for me
four years into celibate sobriety—
no screwing landlords for the happy me
even under a million falling stars
—no stooping low against their trusting wives—
not for Jack or Larry, not even, never

In the brilliant mornings I would get you ready
the bus stopping at the foot of the rutted adobe
Taos air—brilliant cold
no deceitful clutter
no centrifugal men
my sewing machine earned our living
along with sweeping up for Dr. Jack and cooking
Sunday blintzes brunch at the Apple Tree in town
I was proud of paying the dentist
sending you skiing in the Sangre de Cristos
you carried kindling and stacked wood all year
to earn that pass, the Taos kid's special
we'd leave at 5 on Saturday mornings
first on the road before the plows, adrenalin vision
through small arcs holding us steady

we never slid off that road
driving with honesty and studded snow tires
I'd unlock the cafe and you would ski all day

It was a good beginning for me at 30, you at 5 or 6
when I was looking for love and found it

Bossy Bitches, Beautiful Babes

Regina, the queen of the mountain, it was you
I laughed with at the tottering wives, surviving spouses of the
    old
Taos artists—hats askew, painted skin and red red lips above
expensive wraps, jewels big as pets—fragile-looking women

I worried we would become them—witches alone on property
to die for—you, laughing woman, whose
hair ripples silver to your waist *como el Rio Hondo* over
    smooth rocks

you in your mountains, your handmade homes, adobe bas relief
your jewelry on you and in glass-case museums, you, pricey
with aloneness like dry boulders in the sun, bleached oak and
    crochet work
you, with the rosewood pistol for bears or deranged men

that day in the Taos post office, our trucks parked on wet
    Saturday morning
asphalt reflected mirror-like the blues and whites of Taos skies
your face framed then by *los Sangre de Cristos* in high mass
    lace
we had everything and nothing to fear and nothing and
    everything to fear
our kids can only guess at what it was

back then, edgy women, we nudged and bulldozed boundaries
smashing man-made cages of rules to breathe into our very
    own lungs
and inhabit ourselves to own, at least, a chance at living.
You with your cowgirl buckskins beauty to incense Maude
    Gone and half the planet
your laughing lament is now for your poet, the one who would
    bedevil

himself or herself over your raging locks and mad Irish eyes—

you, high on the mountain charming grandkids horses cows
    bad-ass dogs
say you wait still for your perfect mate and I am annoyed.
Mr. Right about as likely as Superman to pay your mortgage
    and cook your steak

Where is the Original Lois Lane today? Tottering into the PO
next to Julia Roberts to complain that Clark was a wuss?
Tell him "I'm here, I'm here, in riches or debt, til death yada
    yada."
Spill it out, Ms. Alphonse Mucha's senior poster girl! So very
    beautiful,
still.

Your Mr. Right's a bit hard of hearing. Eternity's winding
    down the long adobe drive
my dear queen of the mountain, so close to heaven with those
    pretty pretty
horses for friends.

Miki

You have an echo running inside: We want Oreos, Oreos,
    Oreos not arroyos, Mom
and then, not now. We want GI Joes, new clothes, Barbies and
    babysitters—

not, back then: root cellars, rose hip jellies, strings of chilies,
    peyote tipis,
hippie feathers, beads, *rios*, and well-water chaos

Mewling like newborns in huge blind bodies they complain
about the loss, how the rearing you gave them was
    uncomfortable at times

and you remember, to me, your husband's insistences, his
    disappearances and
you remember his belly and his smell, before he lumbered
    away

with that cute nurse back to her life in Florida as he wanted
her life, not his, and not yours

Some kids followed, others scattered like marbles on a plate
and they complain, now, about the scary edges of life without
    you

being cold sometimes and how you didn't save them
from it all, back then, not now

Now they have it all and you didn't do it
They did, alone, and for themselves

and from the loftiness of now
they say you weren't enough back then

to make them mindfully happy now
not enough, at any rate, to share with you, their mother

Dear Michael, Vallecitos, 1971

In the cabin that spring soon as I was pregnant
you took up with Light-haired Sandy—
the men started dropping by just to see
hoping I was loose since everyone knew
I was a fool, not knowing you did
whatever you did with her—she,
strawberry blonde, all about her hair
creamy skinned and flat-bellied—
brain-dead as a milk can but that didn't stop you

When Denny showed up instead of you one night
I still didn't get it—he
mentioned how with you in town a lot
—he, Light-hair's step-brother-in-law
he'd been wondering, but
I had no desire for him or
a dose of trouble with his gang-y girlfriend
Light-hair's step-sister, Dark-haired Sandy
I may as well have fallen on my sword
dark-hair would've cut me up like a jackass
in barb wire

Geronimo found reasons to check on his cows
all winter milling around the valley most of which was his
but him and me, no way—his 60-something
wife Amalia would've shot me right through the eyes
had him bury me without a single fare thee well
besides, he was old—

he parked his truck and
asked me to walk on sheet ice with him one day
though I could see the plan, he grabbing my arm
as I inevitably slipped

Fermin, of course, had come calling

well before your indiscretion—
telling me at the woodpile how much we'd need, how
winters in Vallecitos were nothing to make light of
I snubbed him every time I had to pass his house on
the back way to our place in the valley below

one sunny day after walking the high road in,
to check the mail buy tortillas at Willy's,
say hi, maybe, to the Sandys
going home, Fermin jumped out from a big boulder
He held my arms and shook me a little
as if I were a piggy bank. "Oh for God's
sake, Fermin,—stop it!" I pretty easily twisted out of his grip.
He asked me then could he and a few of his cousins
come down to the cabin and rape me some night.
"No," I answered carefully
learning a shit load about his culture in that one question
"No, I wouldn't like that" I looked right at him,
my eyes each an open blade
he looked down in hat-holding posture, "Ok," he said
"I thought maybe you'd want us to do that. Are you sure?"
"I'm sure," I told him, as if summoning up
the teacher voice inside me
I could finally hear her in the quiet of that canyon
Perhaps she had said yes lifetimes ago
to the wrong man, and I was getting the second chance

What I loved so much about you, Michael
was your smile lying next to me or,
alone, I loved the rose hips, the creek
cascading around sunny boulders
into shady Aspen groves
Jesus, even beavers at the meadow
where we first camped
I was grateful for the men who took no for an answer—
no one spoiled that place for me, not even you

Delirious (a ghazal)

the jug of red wine at my feet the source of it all, the warmth of
    men in exile
alone without family, I followed this man, followed his friends
    in exile

the cold pick-up truck on a San Francisco morning, Nick,
    playing blues and
harmonica tunes like Blind Lemon Jefferson, Willy McTell,
    notes to bend in exile

guitars plucking dawn crooning, someone's percussion and air,
    my own voice silent
Maria, Tina, Janis, leaning into soul, rhythm, rock n roll
    women sweetened in exile

following sound, the pied piper's girls, nowhere to go, nothing
    to be
pungent hashish and ganja for mood, reviling education the
    trend in exile

to make me happy, he said in sea-blue eyes, your work, to keep
    me happy
I fled in a rainy night, headed south to the City, trusting each
    rhythm in exile

Remember, Merimée, from beaches to green chile bursting
    with seed, desert willow
satisfaction, the scrub oak of truth, each longing for
    containment deepened in exile

Star Struck

I duck my head out looking again at stars
like giant tapioca balls dotting the dark ceiling
each one a memory of Southwestern desert

Again ducking into Georgia's house one last chance
to stand in the light show bombarding me with time
under permanent skies. Star struck, I tuck in emotions

OK, not the madness of regret, or freezing
in my footsteps like seeing Johnny Cash in the
Española Shop n Stop, before 7-11
and late night stores ever happened

June Carter stood in heels and a Jackie Kennedy coat
clutching her purse, smiling at my predicament,
watching me watch her husband buy smokes
1970-71 before
I was really pregnant with my star-crossed son—

I, aware, suddenly, of the finger smudges of stove-black
on my yellow velvet bell bottoms made from cast off drapes
and the sweater someone had draped on me that I claimed
always looking for something to be mine, a space, a place,
one star whose shine I could call my own

her smile struck me, my own June Carter smile
tossed in empathy, a favor to another wayward
woman completely gone over her man

Three-Bucket Bath

a long sloping pasture to the river
across one ditch then down along the barbed wire fence line
the easiest way
galvanized buckets and a plastic jug—two people to tote
a 3-bucket bath
pour one into the washtub by the stove
another shower-like, squatting under your lover
who bends over pouring, dangling a hand-rolled cigarette
from his sweet lips
soak up, soap, splash
shampoo and pour slowly again
could be 30-below in bright-white light
the third bucket gives your skin a glow
half a minute of wet-skin New Mexico morning bliss

the old cook stove heats the cabin
our clear plastic door, inside the heavy keep-out-the-bear affair
welcomes the sun bouncing back across the valley
two tiny windows set into logs older than our grandparents
leak a little air, we didn't know to care
didn't think to re-chink mocha-colored adobe filling

Fermin came down that fall to tell us
about the winter, how we'd need lots of wood
asked his curious, hat-crumpled questions

Geronimo brought a sheep and left us with half
packed in the blue trunk in the north-side snow
we had no idea how much we didn't know
all we could do was stoke the firebox
and keep each other company under
piles of quilts on your big iron bed from California

the week our son came into us it was 47 below
the beginning of just about everything
that winter in Vallecitos, 1971

Women finally spoke up in the seventies

quiet in the sixties, still didn't tell; we boomers compliant;
lots of good girls taught serve and smile
Girls these days drop the kiss-up face, whoa baby!
the grinning Mona Lisa and all her being nice. Back then: Oh,
    my body?
Yes, sir. I'll be right with you; my brain, my life? I'm yours, I
    guess.
Did our mothers know? Did they know raising a generation
of *revolucionistas, las feministas locas*?
a Hail Mary off the dead end of servitude, a catapult
out of solitude from a home not ours, but his;
we need attitude to achieve that stance. Thank you, Mom.

We unbound our breasts, let down our hair,
swirled in dance with the Earth bare feet—
we learned to give to ourselves, talk back 'n take no prisoners
—well, almost. We almost won, anyway.
My father rarely held a child, cooked a meal, swept the floor,
    ironed shirts.
He mistook his penis for a power tool, a pliable key to
    ownership
admission to top colleges and jobs. It was a man's world and
we of the fifties, sixties, seventies, we were girls
then "ladies," then bra-burning-bitches, women. Our daughters
    want
choice and pleasure in love and work;
women now yell, tell, and press charges. Our voice,
we want power pricks to put away their killing tools;
to love our mother Earth, no duh. Civilized, my ass! Our kids
    need
food and jobs not replacement parts—we women of the
    seventies
are done with naked emperors, bargain-basement atrocities
America, you are a woman, don't take it lying down—
don't let them scare you into silence, again. Don't be polite,
    again.

Strong Draw Memories

for me it's the Jedediah Smith River Canyon
that thundering course an un-jaded
will to continue
I'd crane my neck to
see out the zooming car California to Oregon
or visa versa
the snake of downhill rapids
bound by sun-touched boulders and
leaning shoulders of cliffs
craggy above
tight-pocket curves

seeking baptism I'd jump in
forgetting, once, to gather clothes, shoes, purse—
that time on Mt. Hood I stood alone under
an icy deluge rebirthing myself
or was it just a need to wash

a frightened person from the car
wrapped me warmly in a blanket but
we both forgot everything I'd
set on the stones by the pool

It was spring in the sixties and my stuff
got boxed and sent by a stranger
to my parents' house Can you imagine the response?
They ran an add in the Portland paper:
"Please call home"
this, after disowning me (Do not come
home they had said not long before)
for living with
that gorgeous man, the blonde who wooed
with mountains and rivers
his life force the most powerful draw at the time

In the Closet with Larry Bell

I designed him the Italian collar, made his shirt
pale fine pink broadcloth from Santa Fe
followed broad shoulders to his huge walk-in closet
for the jacket I would alter
down the blood-poured adobe hall
into his bedroom and this room-size closet for a fitting

my eyes stuck on his one hundred pairs of shoes
lined up on tilted racks
thinking of my son's best and only wear-ables
we got by on so little
I imagined my son, later, having excess too

he tried on the blazer
explaining the shoes
he had been poor
I pinched the would-be tucks
smoothed my hands down each lapel
he slipped his hands over mine
each palm gloving my hand, rooted in easy current
his gaze as if women too belonged, in excess

I dropped my eyes, we both knew
I wouldn't be another jacket on his rack
not even a cashmere, not even a perfect fit
turning as if nothing occurred, taking this
moment as gift—the sculptor and the seamstress

Hairdos and Tattoos

You got a Mohawk when yr first sister was born
ran away for your 13th birthday
five weeks later I found you nested
in a friend's garage
your dad was long gone and I with a new
husband had a baby. You & I fought
over dishes and you never came back
but for your birthdays
chocolate cake laced with your drugs
I didn't hate you for that. You came around.
Remember when u turned 18, all the incarcerated kids
—a little piece for everyone?
How we spent on a lawyer then you chose Springer
so you could smoke instead of waiting at YDDC?
Remember we strong-armed you into our car
so we could help you?
How you never stuck around for help?
How much you wouldn't talk?
How I bought your LSD, flushed it while you watched, at 12?
How you drank Jimson weed tea
Remember swinging at me when I was pregnant?
I'd scared you with screaming? Maybe you were 11?
Remember the flowers you'd bring me
u all chained and tattooed, black leather skinhead friends?
How Brad or Marty threw up in your room
I made them wash the futon cover?
How you stood on a corner and told
me you were going to propose to yr GF?
How I spoon fed you in the hospital
with that tumor in your belly?
How we bought the tiny trailer
so you could have a space?
How you drank a bottle of rum and
turned your intestines inside out right after surgery?

How you brought home the pit bull that I had forbidden
and he ate my pin cushion? You paid for x-rays, not I.
How we all loved him?
How she called me on New Years and asked if I'd accept her?
I was surprised but not surprised she wasn't sober
When she showed up with a slap mark asking me
I said to head north and never turn back
to cover her tracks. How mad you were?
How you'd use smack, crack, whatever
maybe not in that order.
How didn't she know you were an addict?
How you didn't know? How I didn't know.
How she stuck with you after rehab?
How rehab helped save you for your daughter
who missed you so much? And then your son
How you are so blessed
"Grandma, do you know where my dad is?"
Do you remember being happy?
In the dome; at Larry Bell's; at Lotta Burger in Taos?
M-80s on the 4th of July? The cops confiscating one
and you kept one for later?
Do you remember our wedding and your little white suit?
Grandpa? How I so wanted you to go to school? Anywhere?
How much you resented everything?
How you cried in the D-home? How you wanted to go home
but never felt at home with us?
How all you felt was lost and bad, a bad boy?
You found your father and loved him best you could?
How he still disappointed you?
How much you don't want to be him?
Do you remember his eyes, his turquoise eyes?
How tall he was? Fried chicken Friday?
How he was happy sometimes and
loved you in ways you remember?

My Burque Come From Poem

I come from quick marriages before the War, the second war to
    end all wars
each marriage a mini-war as if a child of this desperation
I come from Irish Californians and German chocolate cakes;
from carriage, auto, bike mechanics and teachers,
from preachers and alcoholics and mean sons-a-bitches
I come from Gold Rush, artists and millenary shops,
from big-hatted photographs in open air Cadillacs
I come from El Camino Real and Eucalyptus trees,
a thousand sandy beaches
from moving in the night from bankruptcies
everything left behind
from logging camps and men who whistled at girls
I come from tidy houses to which women were married
from too many children, no seat belts, no mention of love, no
    hugs
from drinking and driving as normal,
from kitchens with a cookie drawer,
a bread drawer, a cigarette drawer,
from gin fizzes on Christmas morning
from hating my body and starving by choice;
I come from having no voice
from booze above a fridge full of glass milk bottles left at the
    door
I come from black and white,
when lies were better than truth,
from sin and hell from revolutions so quick
they stacked up like dominoes;
I come from rock n roll as salvation and
Chuck Berry in a little club half empty in Oakland
from make love not war and gallons and gallons of Gallo
from Mance Lipscomb, Jim Kweskin, and Joan Baez
from a dozen years of pot from embroidered rugs
stuffed with hash from Afghanistan

from cast iron pans and my life in a backpack
I come from turning on and dropping out
I come from boyfriends on heroin
from being taught to be passive
from vets in my bed from Nam and Korea
from the very first waves of acid up and down the Coast
from being entirely lost in empty houses with empty arms
from babies with no fathers or families
the un-wed mothers' wing of a cold Catholic hospital
from food stamps and welfare and a child to live for
from finding *nuevo mexico* where family matters
where the sky is so big and the sun so strong
adobe houses with hollyhocks and blue morning glories
from tuning back to education so my son could have a chance
I come from wanting romance— from teaching and writing
from growing veggies and sewing
from piggy bank dinners and just getting by
I come from everything points toward love
everything points toward the riches inside
from home birth happiness and true love not easy
from the path with joy as divining rod,
the joy in your gut—what does it say?
I come from Giant Sequoias and women not knowing
women whose lives were violent and too often, silent

Upon the Occasion of Punky Color
August 2000

raspberry-sorbet spotted towels and gloves
the deed is done
from roots to tips
shiny, fluffy, the sheen of rip-stop nylon
your hair is excellently not-so-normal now
not that brownish-blonde color of rich honey
glowing streaks god made
but zinnia wild, a chrysanthemum riot
a pink in-your-face
butterfly landing zone
flower power personified
and I, your mother
love your hair dyed
as I love your hair not dyed

mariposas seek solace and sustenance
on heads like yours

hummingbirds will want from you
the sugar that sends them zinging

you send me zinging
you do

Ms. Bobbitt's Bloody Sacrifice

When I heard the story about the penis, severed, carried
and tossed into an intersection—I have to admit to abdominal
Glee! Things would change and they did.

I never see her face or hair; I see her hand, holding the dripping
    member like she'd
hold the stick from a melting Dove bar—a pretty hand,
    upturned, waiting for
the perfect moment to toss, unobserved by militant anti-
    litterists

And as she swung her SUV to the right, a flick of the wrist
    rolled it left, into the gutter. Plop!
like a baby bird fallen in a windstorm, landing dead on the
    sidewalk—pink, a round soft blob—harmless now,
    unattached. No one kicked the penis; no one ran over or
    stepped on it.

Did she intend for it to revive, alone in the gutter? Mercy.
Her head must have cleared once the thing was done, the deed
    of taking his sex,
a sex not given, a sex not consenting

She must have beaned him hard, a frying pan, cast iron? and
then with a blade sharp enough for the rape of multitudes, she
    sliced
through his drunken slumber and settled the score. No more
    would he

insist: prod, shove, push to give what she had not wanted. He
    would have
no way now, to intrude, to claim her space for his. She
    dismembered him

and I felt liberated—a heinous crime in my name too. And yes,
    in '94, New Mexico conceded,

went belly up, that body of legislating men, a man might no
    longer rape his wife with impunity. The courts ruled from
    1994 on, no longer could he bully, nag, and force her.
Most could see now, the risk; their own little penises behaving
    better already.

Women clamored to revile her, of course, as women do; she'd
    gone way too far. But in the halls and rooms without men
    we laughed, a good many of us. One woman, one knife,
    one self-defining act; gutsy, she fought back for the tens of
    millions who have had to acquiesce.

Funnily Enough

for charlie milhaupt

Yes, *funnily*; I finally looked it up
thinking to have one up on you
but funnily, it is an adverb, one which forever
makes me think of you, funny, like when you

talked about flying from Spain to Fire Island for a party
and the Senegalese water taxi dude
had you walk across waist-high water, suitcase and shoes held
    high
your tie perhaps just skimming the city block or so to shore
the dark water flickering beach house reflections

funnily, the party was the next night anyway—

The hurricane howled against sheet-glass windows
As you regaled us that night
but we didn't move, fixed, I'd say, to your story

Funnily enough, you wrote later that our visits kept you going
friends did stop dropping by
Christmas alone with the fever at 105° waiting for a dinner
    promised
by Howard; you said he did show up, finally—a couple of
    years of this

you in New York, us in New Mexico
too far apart, but the wires worked well, funnily

And that last summer at The Pines, we sat on the gray
    weathered deck, close; it was time to go
You were luminescent, your eyes so open, so fatless on your
    Bowie-like face

so surprisingly round like tiny dessert plates of hand-blown
    glass, blue, and of course, Italian
You were beautiful, funnily enough, so thin and pale under
    your tan
with no need to speak of death; you really didn't care for un-
    fun plans

Now, anyone says "funnily" and I see that freckled face,
    leaning forward, half-smiling,
above your white terrycloth robe, your eyes reflecting the bay,
    that happy thatch of dirty blonde hair
so California, still so Hollywood, still you—in striped-blue
    pajamas, or pale blue vapors or
walking on water, funnily enough, if you really wanted to

In Retrospect

I am grateful for the strife like silver bullets
my kids have delivered up close
when they stab my control hand
bite at loose assumptions
drain soupy love like helium
their lovely teeth demonic in funhouse faces
in tinny voices they have hurled concoctions
from cauldrons of childhood meltdown
mirrored separation and poverty
emptied me
seeing myself in them no argument
recognition no claim to ownership
it's a holiday thank goddesses

divine gratitude fills like the meal
we play scrabble and extreme croquet
laugh at the pets and bemoan our electorate
gather to heap blame in the gravy and the hope
of it, carnal drips of cranberry devour
demons as we laugh with chasers
of painful punch and whine for a few
shrill or deep we harmonize
feel our skin like
puzzled survivors and play
to protect those among us

holidays provide ballast
test the bulkheads of daily sunrise
shore up determination
to scatter peelings lightly
into compost, the coinage of
life/death love/hate, the witches' brew
we use from a to z

Velvet Couch in a Room with No Curtains
(a pantoum for Charlie and Gretchen)

you sat all day then called to tell
he went to sofa, morphine sleep at last
he so skinny, wide-eyed, wasting
couldn't tell when AIDS would rest

he went to sofa, morphine sleep
Manhattan sky over paper Narcissus
AIDS, rude game, never shouted "uncle"
small Village penthouse, his upturned palm

Manhattan lights through paper Narcissus
Empire State's red spire on black
Village penthouse an upturned palm
did spirit fly or burst to pure bright white?

Spired Empire red against night
you called at 3 our brother gone
did spirit fly or burst to pure bright white?
quietly, you said. Rest, then he was gone.

you called at 3 our brother's gone
we watched him all day into night
quietly, you said. He rested then was gone.
you, Yanni, Wayde were dark and still

with him, the blue-eyed blonde, so skinny
you, Yanni, Wayde hearts beating, still
sitting all day you called to tell
we surrounded him until his spirit's flight

La Edad Tercera

The vantage point is lofty, the river far and
winding green, a long climb from the sixties

Serenity and suffering resolve
when the last third starts at sixty

You on the cliffs damned sexy in the
sailor's turtleneck, velvet bells: knit sixty, purl sixty

Oh, you men of the ocean—the gifts given
add to a breezy sixty

Cold days, hot, cold decade
hot times six equals sixty

Don't beg run or ask
silly me, stuck again; sixty over sixty is one

Stubborn self, will you learn for a nanosecond
the sixtieth of a strike of light

That time is now, Merimée, arranged like
tulips swaying, multi-colored, sixty or so, at least

old black sheep

twenty years of abandonment
then found
brought home by his son
broken, needing everything

I didn't like how he looked at me
resentful, angry about something
but later that summer
meeting him when I dropped off my grandchild
our grandchild
his arm swung up around my waist
and we went down the driveway together
the twenty years forgiven
they hadn't been intended to hurt

that moment, together in one spot
hips, arms, legs moving as one
his dying body a few years ahead of me
we held our sides to each other firmly
all that was allowed, one walk
a chosen walk, a how-I-do-love-you-still walk

Burque Ghazal

at her yard-sale Sarah carried blue Willow china. Mood: in the
    groove
Nadine's stuff vintage, varied, sleeves of vinyl blues in the
    groove

1963 club in Eugene, upstairs on rain-wet Willamette St. Kathy
    showed
me musicians, night life, my inner needle attuned in the groove

twenty years in the trenches young writers revolve positions
set hands to writing, enticing the muse, kick off shoes in the
    groove

Miki buys green Adriatic figs in Santa Fe with red-jam insides
can we woo our selves skinless, a delicious spoon into the
    groove?

America the beautiful, lost your shiny penny did you? Get
    loose
with Liberty, rebel up, swoon by twos in the groove

O poets of Burque, expounding ancient soothsayer tones
progeny of mile high families sound true in the groove

my culture spattered across land, skittles spinning lazily to fall
misogynist Irish slaves to money and booze in the groove

sons and daughters bless me doubly rich, my family knit
by hand and sweat, I salute you wholly, cruise in the groove

so, Merimee, hips and huzzahs in watermelon wooly sun
make love not war defines the word, soothing in the groove

Ode to the Chevy on a Stick

I ride my bike, brief exercise to: Surprise! Chevy on a Stick
Public outcries! Blue and aqua tiles, the Chevy on a Stick

Our mother would wake us, no lolling about like artists
Rise n shine, sleeping beauties, whole bevy. On the stick!

Giant redwoods, dusty roads wrap cavernous yawps, log
truck drivers, at the sawmills, little Yeti on a stick

Baby, when you're hot you wanna shift my gears
pant and kiss, sometimes lean so heavy on the stick

That little coupe, me next to you in soothing rain
shadowy curves on misty roads, ocean taffy does the trick

Don't wait, Merimée, stiletto blood of your namesake, your
pen in Corsican grass, plume stomping steady on a stick

Recycle under Zia suns, the best stuff grows from cracks
flourishing in corn rows, our dessert, the Chevy on a Stick

Lessons during Birth

Did you get a picture of our hands, Mom?
Your eleven-year-old boy paw
open on blue quilt, your face
pleading for inclusion

you and I rode tigers into town
ferocity the close-held coin
not much to spare
on your unfurling wants

Her tiny girl hand
clutched your fingers
I sold my Riverside Shakespeare
for you; paced behind bars

your step-dad's letting me down
no huge surprise
his mind so often on the job
the game the
power of manly intention

Her birth took time inside my skin
my marrow sought a balance point
you brought me ice, kept
your face close, spent boy whispers
on your soon-to-be sibling

more than bare bones necessity
you connected to the fine art
of setting your sister down
noting her moment of birth

his hands helpless in pockets like
an old-school dude jingling change
to remind us of his everything

mathophilia

I had a math teacher
taught that crazy
geometry without lines and rulers
not a protractor in sight
air geometry
long proofs
after three terms of calculus
(the surface area of donuts
you know—
how many gallons of glaze for the town's
daily dose) when to release a projectile
oh that's vector analysis
point and release
but this professor was hot—
worst womanizer I
adored. Each class he'd
step up on the dais
eating a Snickers in jeans
& rolled up sleeves
leather vest, rode a Harley
played guitar, told us
he'd read our pitiful proofs
over the weekend
none of us geniuses
he'd pick out a tune
wander around his dining room
Number crunchers he said.
Not a brilliant mathematician
in the bunch. I wanted to be under him
on his office desk
but even that I didn't want.
His lectures filled boards with proofs
he talked and talked
I, transfixed and hot.

He had that tough appeal, deep voice
shaggy graying hair and a phd
His final one on one
in his office
the proof of a theorem he'd propose—
an hour of chalk with his eyes
burning my back
everything in a shakey strong
hand laced with sex
I didn't want enough
no nice panties or sexy bras—
too married, a love-doped mama
I never looked til
he shook my hand
he'd be around he said
(if I changed my mind)
I could drop by he smiled
—no cheating, got my A
he an enemy to my married state
and the geometry
a fucking waste

American Ghazal

It's the thought of starting over—the seed of being
rushed in waves from now to there, the cry of a baby

out of control, cribbed, bibbed, flailing for food
sheer waste to worry that I might be, still, far from you, babe

so long my lap a pedestal for the wealth of nations, glorious
    toddler flesh
sweet thighs beyond Swift's dreams, a wild ecstasy of holding
    babies

you ask where I will return and I get miffed—it didn't matter
for so long—you busy with fame 'n rock 'n rollin' other babes

my road became littered with kids via those alluring
aberrant types sporting ga-ga baby blues and bad-ass muscles

and now each breath is a seed of potential—so much
so simple, the act of love, baby, 24/7

and I, poetess, am not alone in seeking truth in
employment. Blah, Blah—Boys blowing stuff up. Babies
    growing up

Why do we miss that brass ring as we go round and round?
Do you remember? Don't ask me, baby, where I'll be

Spontaneous Birthday Poem for Kerry

clear, like crystals in a spring
you laughed at us and with us
summer in summer out
not minding our occasional vinegar for water
you took us: family, home, room
a tent, a place to eat, young and growing
your father home at night whom you shared as if
giving us a rib or two without complaint
camping trips, campus walks, computer classes
round table, 4th of July M80's with Amos
the bad bike ride when the wheel released
you had to hold my hand as they scrubbed
asphalt from your head and face, no drugs
the ride where thugs said your bike
was too crappy to steal-- your back pack
software worth any street deal they imagined
your secret life and the life I saw well merged
good son a blessing without disguise
game playing, joker son baby maker
game making step-son friend Godsend

Summer Son

You arrived like a hockey puck right to my feet
Blam! New son!—no pre-natal, laboring, pregnancy required
little blonde son, suitcase in hand
Perfectly formed, I inspected your nails, your slim fingers
glowing skin, lips laughing at Mad Libs—born to me
age eight, stoic as a cigar Indian, an umbrella of serendipity
We relaxed into our insta-relationshop
like sunbathers relax, snoring lightly in salt air
the curling rumble of the sea, landlocked
desert, I paid you to be quiet
You carried pen and paper, advising
how we could be, checkerboards
and Commodore 64
loving your father ferociously
with generous portions left for me

a poem for my baby

my beautiful Germanic/Irish white honky Anglo gringa
daughter opted for high school in the hood, ours—
felt safe cuz if anything happened, she said, her big brown-
　　skinned
male friends packing would protect her; makes me proud using
　　her
noggin like that—a member of the 16% so-called white kids—
　　she liked
to watch the ranchero dancers on the patio at noon, some of
　　them
would offer to wash the Mustang her rich uncle
dying of AIDS had left her, sent on a truck from New York
the very day he died—happy birthday for all your birthdays
the card said and if u put the pedal to the metal don't tell yr
　　mom

the government could have acted quicker to get
the meds for him & his friends—a genocide of gays unnamed,
most genocides are as they occur. The girl makes friends
and goes everywhere with her inner-city education
the one you get an extra point for
on your college apps, just for surviving.
During the worst blackout in halls with no back up lights
or windows, only one small non-fatal knifing. Not bad
　　considering
the stats and odds of our sickie sick society—and two thousand
　　kids.
There is a thing called happy at that school—
being in your own shoes, the real you is
de rigueur, no fake and falsity required, no pretentiousness
preferred. She was astonished to discover it's ok
to be fat if you're black; we feel better even if we're white—
at least some girls enjoy their real bodies with few teases
about tubby in a tank top to crush her tender heart

my beautiful Germanic/Irish white honky Anglo gringa
daughter travels to foreign lands, multi-cultural is
her home. Adventure is her game. She is my world
and means the world, everywhere, under all constellations.

Big Ms, Little Miss
(a mother's villanelle)

I guess I'm sorry for annoying you
by urging just one taste of vegan fare
black beans and corn, green peppers all askew

I could have skipped the lecture on the food
how vitamins and diet are a care
I guess I'm sorry for annoying you

I'm no purist, preferring chocolate too
sweet sugar blues such an enticing snare
black beans and corn, green peppers all askew

Yes, who am I to nag about the rules
French crepes divine for you and sis to share
I guess I'm sorry for annoying you

The power of legumes so tried and true
my only want strong bones and nails and hair
black beans and corn, green peppers all askew

The sun-trapped might, green and yellow imbue
ancestral gold from Earth's maternal care
I guess I'm sorry for annoying you
black beans and corn, green peppers all askew

Ode to Jane Kenyon

it was the curtain in her
room that made me love
her writing

the view from the bed of
her ceiling

the slowness made me love
her written words

quiet-colored afternoons
soft-feeling time
I loved her lines, soft

fitted sheets and messy crumpled
bed spreads foot-shoved

curtains gossamer-white in
pale blue, bright light

her life in slow
gardening gloves cast on a
chair

the sheer panel lifting through
air in her room

in her life
she wrote of time

open doors

wild honey runs in thick golden rivulets
down to where the trees give shade
where last summer tablecloths
flapped sails under tall
jars kissed with wax
like grandmother's
tree-lined lips

today the trees flap crying
what holocaust has fallen
what holocaust on the ground
where tablecloths held jars of honey
where now Hussein's wife lies bleeding
on three children's gathered limbs

the street runs thick with slivers of things
everyone slipping down to the shade
where last summer tablecloths
held jars of lemonade
where Danai and Omar
played with Arat's
baby goats they too
among the dead

Granai, Afghanistan May 2009

USA bombs village, kills 147 civilians, 0 Taliban

I looked again and again at her eyes
black-burka-framed face exposed
her hand receiving a packet of bills
accepting change
for a husband and two children
crazed eyes
her babies
for millions of seconds alive
her village of quiet nights
festive meals
her gaze now without
smooth curves like satin to fall on
a third cherub with curls
in her arms in soft cotton dress
leather-soled shoes tied nicely
like her brother's her sister's
shoes now minced for landfill
by our unbelievable overkill
can one finger press a button
to bomb the mother's babies
in one second
in one second faster
than birth or conception
they are gone

Before the Apocalypse

I dream up stuff, a job, I want to buy some clothes for the
    apocalypse
you said, "Now there's a poem 'Clothing for the Apocalypse'"

some story of jungles, war in Nam and ". . . Now," the river
boiling horror, "Horsemen (Four?) Apocalypse"?

the New Yorker's annual poster board cartoon
old gloom's "Extinction"; tut tut, we deplore apocalypse

your roses last for days then droop, not a wasted gesture
each years' beauties add to our bouquet: no floral apocalyse!

your mouth at times will quiver under mine: lifelong kiss
I the sand, you the water, our shore, a pair of lips

children, barking dogs, decided, we engage
distract ourselves galore— abhor apocalypse

imagine no finery denied, no fear-based henny penny
style assuages, shop to soothe, groove to Calypso hips

each deed each thought and phone call, someone saying
    "Merimee"
I crave a flash, your brilliant eyes, to be adored before
    apocalypse

Cyclops baby

One eye above two cheeks
center aligned above your tiny new-born nose.
Depleted uranium leaves
messages all over your country; dna
bullies threatening mamas and kids regarding a
bad president, indecipherable
little Cyclops, tender
infant feet in the right place,
two legs, two hands, sad single eye,
what will the nurses do with you? You'd
be great in a freak show back here in the
States. Your owners could call you
little freedom baby.

phone call vote against bombing babies
(a pantoum)

last night I thought branches might fall
I saw myself, our house destroyed
the yard tree-lined like bombs deployed
demonic winds might take it all

I saw myself, our house destroyed
the hand with cash, remorseful gall
demonic winds would take it all
the villagers' wild-honey life now void

the US with cash, silver-coined gall
bodies picnics pets husbands toys
the villagers wild-honey life now void
how much to pay for kids so small?

bodies picnics pets husbands toys
collateral damage yet we stand tall
how much to pay for kids so small?
who will be spared the girls? the boys?

collateral damage yet we stand tall
why not like wind raise voice make noise?
who can be spared the girls? the boys?
secure in houses we don't call

why not like wind raise voice make noise?
the yard tree-lined like bombs deployed
secure in houses where we don't call
last night I thought branches might fall

At School Today 2006

a guy holds the door then wants to converse as we walk
just back from deployment breaks through his lips like
sea foam curling up the beach
he's salty with muskrat eyebrows
I search his face for Iraq
say hope u don't get snatched right back
"oh probably will" he muscles off to
collect more education   shells bulge his briefcase
the silent smokers observe us   one-legged seagulls
jealous of my bright-green goose down coat

after class a European tells me his dictator
slaughtered citizens en masse then
rounded down to one hundred sixty
he, a foreign student, won a green card in the lottery
I do not ask to see, says he wants help with English
has a degree not transferable from his dictator's country
he works for the airlines; can't speak freely in his country

in class we hear a homeless poem; homework: a homeless
     poem
on the way to Target the most raggedy-assed bum on the
     overpass
meets my eyes   wind whips his dirty-blonde hair, flak jacket,
     torn pants
I hand him a buck and get a very good rendition of the word
     "sweetheart"
his corporate voice blasts me like Pacific surf, sends me
     tumbling as
I recognize his ocean eyes from another life somewhere
he steps back on the curb I wave like a California girl
he, a beach boy I never knew and for one warm 'Burque
moment, I was not unhappy

the world in a word rant poem

raise yr hand if yr a feminist—okay!
once considered a radical notion—
feminism is again a dirty word (outside this inner sanctum)—
that's propaganda like "you need a hummer" or
gloria's fish needs a bicycle
feminism is four syllables rich, not some puny expletive!

feminism rolls off the tongue like fertility and flirtiness
the silt and sand of the Nile, the hot sun of New Mexico chiles
but "uterus envy"? kind of a clunker—the root of misogyny
waving its wand at you and me—get back, Rosa; get down
    from that
glass ceiling; Hilary—know yr place, nut cracker

Uterus envy schools women into ridiculing ourselves
a five-syllable pre-emptive strike
from those who would have us
silent, compliant like when good girls
didn't tell—when good girls didn't
ask why we paid with our lives
to be his wife

women with voice and confidence are feminists now
our wailing sirens lure, our hair entices yet
feminists do not deny a right choose
anyone's right to ambition
power pricks trick girls into belittling themselves—
advertising the vagina as empty space
no one home?   a nothing until
his presence and only his presence his fleshy key the only key?
feminists can't stay in Rapunzel's tower pining away
wasting their days "Oh, oh, where is my darling prince?"
—back then women coined the motto "Fuck Housework"

not literally sex with door knobs and broom handles, unless, of
    course . . .
Let me deconstruct for you—toilets and washing machines
are not a life's worth of fascinating
pick up your own damn socks was the first step, honestly—ask
    your moms—
males were dropping socks n underwear all over America
until feminists said "No! No more!"
The little lady's job description was to clean up his shit, so lots
    of us
stopped being little and stopped being ladies, and stopped with
    the nice;
feminism brings us "she" and "her,"
women in text books, title IX—
feminism demands my body is mine—
keep your creepy translations of the Bible
out of my womb please and off of his ass—
what a place for the Bible for god fucking sakes
God likes sex, by the way—she invented it!
I grew up with girdles and garter belts
uncomfortable bras, principals/bosses
patting yr ass
no domestic violence laws
—we're not so far
from the Burkas, the chadors
we've come a short way, sisters, in 50 years—
job for job, hers & his, seventy-eight cents on the dollar,
America,
come out of the closet and join the feminist world
revel in womanhood: womanist, feminist, liberty
justicia—proud words
our hope for the future, our world in our words
¡que vivan las femenistas!

Subject line: Steve

death sent me an e-mail on a Saturday afternoon
clearly stated "you've heard, I assume?"
I called the messenger direct—
he barely got his voice in the phone
so empty of friend
the details? voted, watched results
a drift to a coma
ready to roll in a tucked-in Rosie shirt
old guy with
chipped tooth, cleft chin, wide grin

death's passenger left a note
"a yogi next time, the Himalayas"
I replied: Taos
perfect opposites on the globe
as far apart as we can get

death left me an e-mail and I sent out pictures
have you seen this man? recently? he's
liable to show up in your darkened room
slip in through your open heart
upload a photo if you have one

my sister e-d me with condolences
he'd been in her dream
on his back playing guitar
"He looked happy," she said

I envisioned other lovers gone
from me to her but didn't mind;
his flesh long since forbidden
death left me an e-mail about no worries:
the passenger for the Midnight Special
had caught his train right on time

2000 students in 1 minute

Pre-school blondie had eternal diaper rash
Amy arrived with vomit in her hair
one boy came first left last every day—
mom visited on her break, just once—
I see them round town, in classes later
all OK, could be ok-er
x 100
middle-school
Matt called Aracelli "ho"
and I called his mom
Aracelli could do math at the board
Jackson was ready to break Stella's face
she half-white had kicked him in the ass
Jackson's mom called me racist for stopping the fight
Jessie pulled her hair over bruises
mom slapped her hard but not often she said
they all loved King Lear. One set the other's hair on fire
one tried to ignite my bookshelf but
most of them did not: they read, they worked,
they wrote
Hector's dad wouldn't talk or listen
refuges from El Salvador
x1200
high school:
guns, babies, sex, drugs, joy
good work, bad, long-houred jobs
teasing, beating, living, dying
when Rachel pulled the trigger a part of me died—
she was born too beautiful
students watched me cry in every class
that's all I did that day—the news came over the PA
Janae said she hadn't known, until then
that teachers really cared
x 700

hippie goddess gets it right

on Facebook someone posted a goddess hippie sitting in lotus
infant suckling her right full breast
her hair long blonde, thick, her body surprisingly ample
no surprise considering goddesses
not only suckled their young unabashedly
but laughed right out loud at Twiggy;
we were voluptuous, not jealous. Twiggy was cool
we were hot.

Twiggy, brought skinny back in, fashionably thin
severely cocaine and champagne—
we'd never fit the trend: Twiggy?
Today?♥ happy
and alive. She too must've liked her own
milk-filled breasts, all of us smoking ciggies
more or less
ignorant.

We all went naked or half, or a third—big asses, big thighs
after the babies came, we had to get jobs—breasts drove
bosses wild so we got women's lib and harassment laws

I read the news today: nursing babies is radical!
Whoa—those hippies
and the rest of the world had it right—mama milk, groovy
yummy, handy, perfect & outta sight!♥♥
but get this, when you whip out a tit, back then at least,

———————————————

♥ Twiggy is about 64, quite lovely, eats healthy and hasn't yet
had cosmetic surgery. She keeps fit by walking mostly on the
beach with her husband of many years.

♥♥ Call La Leche League if you ever need encouragement with
nursing.

before Lorena, before Anita Hill and Clarence who lied,
fools falling all over themselves
asking for sips, just a taste? Total strangers asking to
please, could they please get in line? Crazy rude salivating
right to your face
stories about never getting any of that—
sweet jaysus, nursing in public is brave, not brazen
sweet mother of god
and the nursing falls on women, no duh
and leaves the men bamboozled--

F-U Bobby Gee

Fuck you, Bobby Gee, raising your voice at me, fat boy.
You look like a really big scared gerbil
in your too tight brown tee-shirt,
trying to intimidate, but I ain't scairt or is that amn't?

Do you think those eyelashes can make up for
homophobic, racist, tiny gerbil balls?
Do you wonder, Bobby Gee, alone in the kitchen
why your girlfriend sleeps around?

Little rodent community-college looser, F U, Gee-boy.
How dare you wait til everyone's gone
to try to get me to say "oh yes, I'm biased.
I hate you and that's why you got a C."

Lucky son of a gerbil to get a C, when you can't paragraph
or make sense out of ten words or pour a bowl of cornflakes.
—Betch you think get the teacher's a really smart game?

Beth cha think you're giving me a thrill
flexing those gym boy muscles all alone after nine—
everyone's left the parking lot—no one but this old lady
an u yelling in my face while I decide not to assault with intent
      to kill—
thumbs to eye sockets "out vile jelly" just for fun—

You're practically crying that no one gets "C"s but u.
Except, see, Bobby Gee, that evangelist homophobe
across the room supports his God-damning us opinions
and writes a good argument.

You just blather, blubber boy, 'bout "The really big fence"
and how liberals get the literature books all to themselves,
and you have to read that "stuff"

When you wrote to Dubya to tell him on me, did you just
dip your gerbil paws in ink and scratch around?

You want a fair representation of hate-mongering dumbass
    writers,
advocates of all the –isms and phobias, I suppose.
What were the editors thinking, leaving out your side?

Listen here, you one-pair-of-pants-owning, gel-styled mama's
    boy,
you annoy me in your stuffed-up snotty way;
you behave just like mommy and daddy taught you—
to think like them and squeek like them. Do they write your C-
    papers too?
You don't speak, Bobby, you huff, puff, and pout.
There's nothing to draw out of you but booger-sized pieces
of boredom you have the gall to call "your opinions"
like you're scared of "those Mexicans," taking your father's
    jobs
and you want that "really big fence" to keep things really
fair and legal—don't cha eyelash boy.

hmmm, Gee Bobby, little brat, I, your teacher,
declare you a cracker-eating hate-radio loving, white-washed,
Rupert Murdoch adoring, show-sucker.
Go stick your finger in your nose and call Bill O'Reilly;
whine about liberal teachers who make you read in college,
    poor thing—

You don't wanna hear the sad truths
notched on our American belts.
You say all my friends were cowards
if they didn't fight in Vietnam,
if we want our troops home now, not later—

but then again, gerbils aren't called on to do that much—
maybe from your cage the only news is a haze of steaming
    gerbil poop.
Bobby Gee, get off the nincompoop list of scary-ass
academic statistics; you've got some learnin' to do,
and I can't help you much more than that.

Forgive Me for this Rant on the Uterine Homing Device

Every time you ask me to find a thing
anything
I will bill you.
Today, for finding the iron, I am
buying myself a skirt at Dillards
with your money.

I theorize that women of your mother's
generation taught sons dependence
on purpose; you weren't to learn how
to find, how to not need us, I suppose,
so women wouldn't be thrown down
the well at birth, so women would have
on-going employment
or at least food and clothing for
their miraculous abilities of not
only putting away and retrieving things
but also living in a state of continual
preparedness to perform such services
at the drop of a fucking hat, and graciously.

Fortunately for us, the "graciously"
part became an anachronism when women
chose education and self-expression
over servitude to preposterously
panic-stricken and assuming men.

Conversations with Women
a haiku series

divorce in the air
older women breaking thru
just stay home he says

she has fun with friends
he's so glum when she has fun
just stay home he says

what's to eat he glares
whatever you want she says
her keys in her hand

caretaking addict
she's his mother wife and friend
her time running out

so easy to please
a damn tree makes her happy
not mis'rable men

all they ever want
mistress housewife pretty thing mom
it's all about them

will I be alone
he neither talks nor listens
I find that quite dull

reality sucks
I'm scared of divorcing
so much junk to toss

the Dalai says judge
success by what you gave up
freedom is a must

free to be happy
to laugh sleep eat write and be
my own life to live

my shoulders in flame
he doesn't see my dragons
my dangerous pets

I want my own life
Virginia wanted a room
I want more than that

your happiness is
not my job get your own life
you make you happy

you can't have my life
my happiness my own problem
you're off the hook

rejoice each day new
a potpourri of choices
you yours, mine for me

Get real. Need me where?
by your side, behind you when-
ever you want what?

crazy magic rich
world of possibilities
listen breathe and see

Georgia my dear friend
a light among bright poets
an inspiration

women will be true
her story unfolds to heal
no turning back now

no silencing us
we carry the seeds, the food
the future is ours

Our Guys

She and I murder our husbands like crows
cackling in times of plenty
They're air bags stopping us from a dangerous away
Boom! You're veering too far—do we get cookies again
Boom—I want to make love, said across the room
you wonder with whom.

Boom! Where are my keys? How much in the bank?
Boom! Let's go to the mountains. What's for breakfast?
Mine isn't cleaning his bathroom these years
leaves pots and pans stacked like Twin Towers
Boom—like a gas they fill the house with him-ness
himism, their him shows and himmy movies—so much
him we run to the hills, to California on a plane or Louisiana
to our rooms, our extra house, our cars
our meetings for those with fucked-up mothers.

They think we do whatever we want; they're wrong
We do what we can from one leap to the next
dance like ninnies around our want, warming our hands
We don't un-choose them; too good to lose
Won't harass them or disappear much;
no insults for hers, she calls him honey
to his face and darling.
I keep mine busy; he needs lots to do
or he just locks up
like a rusty toy.

On the Solitude of Lie/Lay

He is carefully careless about lie/lay
or caring how things lie
announces his position like a child bringing
a flower or identifying a cloud shape
his take on lie/lay ephemeral at best
his choice to let it lie, to let it rest as if the
lay of the land determined usage
yet laying himself down to sleep
lying prone upon his wife-bought bed
today he lies, yesterday he lay, tomorrow
he may lie, may be laid, get laid, or may have
lain in vain awaiting his rarely lying wife
who avows no harm: no lie to love
but not to lie as a mandatory decree
Had he laid a trap
lying in wait like a predator
they might have lain together nevermore
It's choice that lets us lie in
comfort, to lay our heads upon
the pillow along the side of
that body so familiar
one might never guess it too will lie
upon the cooling board, laid by
wife or husband who will never, past
one undetermined day, lie with the body
of that chosen love
who lay just yesterday so close

dialogue

we sit and cry in mother/daughter voices
juggle tell with ask   our life waves crescendo
cathedral-shaped chains and blame
rattle a dance in sense and soul loss and gain
penitentes heading to dark *moradas*
no more solemn in their spiritual task nor
Chaucer's petitioner offering poems to the court
nor Catholic memories of stained glass saints
their backs arched to curve of sun-filled window
we hold light, a tear-stained prayer for grace
linked by birth I wish I'd given you keys
to unlock now a three part harmony
to open everything to heart fire
to know a rest stop, to wake up at once
in a bright morning of being:
smooth-worn stones on perfect paths
lines of jubilant, New Mexico
cream puff clouds, pink as
watermelon

In Whole Foods

the guy at the table in front of me is an
old hippie/cowboy with thick silver ponytail

a cashier walks over to him and this plain
woman glows as if her lights had been dimmed

seems this man just threw the switch allowing
beauty to soften her skin with color

suddenly everything about her is love for him
her plain black baggy tee shirt, loosely caught hair

non-descript jeans from nowhere become
a disguise. I can see she only dresses and

undresses for him, just this one, he with a few
feathers like a peacock in his attire. His tee-shirt

his pants hung just so, a little pretty, this guy
to attract his prize. She smiles at him

lovers making plans
even if married some 20, 30, 40 years

then she is back at the register
one more look while making change

Underage Mom   *For Vanessa*

The cashier averted her eyes and muttered
"You should be her sister not her mother"
You leaned into her space as if saying
I am fiercely her mother
how dare you confuse my daughter
She shows me off like a trophy
Are you a hater of the young? you could've said
Do you mete out shoulds like dirty pennies

Daring your walls to burst, I watched you take her insult
knowing you are your daughter's Lake Havasuu her Yangtze
you are the power that gets her roof and tiny skirts, her books
and parks, her parties, braids, and shoes. You cook for her
you are her listener her singer her washerwoman
some afternoons, her friend You bring home the everything
You hold your daughter in a love haters only dream of
"You should have held your tongue,"
you think to her, "you should have sewn your lips with
thick green twine" you think to her
your fingers ache with venom toward her blind teeth
this crazy woman wants to unchoose you from your job
to give you more suicidal, bored, and ravaged teenage years
wanted you to do without the child the goddess sent
wanted to steal from you the divine gift you protect
while she sacks your groceries

that woman could've thought of golden apricots
could have thought of quesadillas and gorilla books
might have known that she too has life to give
but she forgot, she forgot to breathe
forgot to give anything but grief to you

Let's wish like witches, a baby to her womb
Let's wish a sweet-smelling head of curls onto her breast
a cherub cheek beyond her stinging limitations

Miki in the Mountain

We both changed our minds regarding arguing
not so good at it after all
I followed you south in 1970
a frying pan in my pack, a dog at my feet, I
wanting to see through your eyes again
ate bologna sandwiches with green chile
never doubting I'd find you
No phones back then, but the PO
the grocery store—places you
would frequent; I found you in desert and sunshine
Your well with a bucket out your kitchen door
your wooden outhouse in hard dirt chamisa
nestled in sage, scrub oak, salt cedar, piñon
You at home, not surprised I'd follow you a thousand miles
—New Mexico someone had said, El Rito,
but I found you in Hondo, happy
with the ditch gate open, on your knees in the row
weeding, covering with straw, plants to fill
your Oz-like root cellar, jars and jars,
boxes of fruit, goods to see everyone through;
irrigating your terraced hillside garden with unclear
fertile, green-tea river water, ditch water, everything pliable
The house two stories adobe big cook stove roaring
just warm enough—kids running on dusty oriental rugs
screen door slamming, children chasing
in the yard and through the back door
Your blue-eyed husband in constant motion
eyeing women who envied you. You had a home, pueblo style
a sewing room, sewing machine, a closet, a riot of jewels,
    blood and earth tones, every texture of fabric, cool, poured
    adobe
floors. Miki, little gypsy Roma woman, dark hair waving
    down
Your bloodline black-clad Hungarian smokers at grand pianos
ignorers of children, gave you a nanny—
you, in your motherhood fed your minions and millions

kettles of beans, pans of corn bread, your kitchen an open and
    free café
You catered to me, you cared for me: Sister, Mother

I go to you, hold what needs holding and follow you again.
Somewhat humbled by your revelations—
my uppity attitude, my bent to instruct to
correct your diction and syntax. How funny, in the end
we parted over word choice
me smoothing your hair properly
our goodbyes. Adios, mi hermana,
little pal too tender for my tone
how I loved to laugh with you. Thank you.
True there were days I felt smarter, richer
prettier; foolish me
forgetting that through your eyes I was an
interloper scrounging for a word to push me along
something from your stores,
clandestine veggie and dry goods distributor

You kept the change, then change hit you like a storm
all power out, husband gone
baby making over, the end of that sweet Hondo song.
You branched out to silver and gems, women friends,
Santa Fe lovers who gave you pleasure you said
kids would visit as you moved
place to place, always your own pace and proud
your own woman until the down hill, slide to the end.

We went to the river, we went to Gap and J Crew
I weaned you from my wallet when the money ran out, and
you weaned me from you, knowing I would be alone.
On the mountain, today, they are digging a grave to lay you in
ground hard as granite and full of quartz
You have set them a task to honor your wishes
to celebrate your past, your life,
your joy you did not hoard but shared with us.

Portland Reminds Me of You

The night I was a cat burglar dressed all in black
I found a frying pan and a cutting board; then
the night spit us into a car
up the dark wet Portland street to home.
Abandoned stuff, old residential rooms
Ruined two-burner hot plates; all kinds
of splintery falling plasters and lathe.

Our friend did this for a living and wanted to share,
like an actor inviting us to see his play, a poet her performance
no poets performing in my Portland then.
Just buttermilk bars and old Jewish bakeries, the colleges
and art schools for the civilized young, the ones who
could think in long straight lines, listen and know
how to be in the straight groove of life. Ten
years of crooked was fully enough.
Cars that started, houses that held, friends
who were, all of that happened. Just
the deviation when rock n roll took
over, and funny drugs and jugs of wine, old trucks
with singing men playing instruments and
I learned to listen, to listen and dance,
to dance and want, to need one thing
then another, especially for my son. He changed me
that boy. For him I would walk the line
of thoughts and plans and days with work,
too alone to call it fun; then fun came along.
The frying pan and cutting board still
in my kitchen, the man at my side, the laughter deep
from the gut, ready enough to gurgle up,
abundant, artesian.

Girlfriends the absolute value of necessity.
Even at your death, we laughed as you knew

your body was taking a final bow.
The trick it was laying on you of
shutting down, one switch at a time,
like all those empty hotel rooms, your organs
bones muscles blood skin face hair letting go the
chi and your prettiest smile hooded over the
evacuation, utterly out of your control.

Travel Poem for Leens and Ursi Winter 2011

Paris—beheadings for wrong living, wrong doing, wrong
  being, gold plated glory

Paris—thin women, thin-legged men, black coats, small space
  taking, narrow chairs

Paris—shopping for the rich, the masses, necessities and haute
  couture, Lena leads

Paris—brick, stone, plaster, frescoes, iron roses, marble,
  granite fortress with a moat

Paris—my marriage loose ending as if a whip tail unattached—
  the solution? museums

Paris—my daughters, bonding jagged edges, we move on,
  brisk in frigid temps

Paris—cafes, the metro, Pont Neuf, the euro, reminders of my
  generous brother

Paris—an inheritance in café au laits, creamy sauces, pastries
  to die for at every turn

Paris—family welcoming, and we them; we suffer less, the
  French, says my French ex-nephew

Paris—while friends worry about food and heat, I am dining
  out in Paris

Paris—my veggie soup several meals, gruel, bread, cheese,
  quinoa salad from the Bio

Paris—we follow Ursula to Istanbul—to say in Turkish: hello,
  goodbye, and thank you

Year of the Rhododendron, a Rainy Day Ghazal, or Trust Yourself

I'm in Oregon, gingerbready untethered thinking
Hydrangeas, Rhodies, palms rub together thinking

In al-anon, we seek serenity in sober camaraderie
like lovers oaring boats toward sunnier thinking

thin rich women walk a birds-of-paradise line
tease the gaze to unravel, to unfetter thinking

vintage evangelists hiss, spoon caffeinated venom
at America's cup of vulgar thinking

United Fruit Company fertilizes lives with lives
citizens for bananas, poster-pretty unfair thinking

ping pong spreads like trumpet vine, our golden
climate changed, smaller exercise, newer thinking

repetitive agony a distant rumble, science dour
remove pesticidal irritants, forego sour thinking

splendid days Merimée succinct in orange, the silk net
grape-shaped voluminous, bellows tap tap tap your thinking

A Veggie-ghazal

I'm always cooking up bowls of spinach
even asking in restaurants for bowls of spinach

spinach and eggs, chicken, spanikopeta
a landscape of gardens sown of spinach

are we to question Popeye's love potion, Olive?
Goddess-driven swampy oceans of spinach

Hepatitis non A, non B, but C: The gift of her
illness springs to greet, sassy soul of spinach

opposite divine her eyes writhe green
envy the sound the groan of spinach

flutes oboes cello horns sing Dvorak
oh sweet virtuosos so extol the spinach

words lifted from Emily, her predilection for white
no washing day dye for that glow of spinach

do you recall the vows to be happy or change
we'd bend to each other, be homegrown spinach

who would guess we'd outlive the battle, the race
unknown to the finish; our life, yes, prone to spinach

that moment remains impressed on my breath, you
potent and promising grassy earth betrothed of spinach

today, as planned, you execute an omelet: creamy
bacon bits, hmmmm, yes, in the zone of spinach

Oh, Merimée, would you spin again a web for him
the one who loves you in his home of spinach

the *NYTimes* reports

a female Komodo dragon
given enough solitude and celibacy
can clone herself: each hatchling
an identical agave green
her satisfaction shared in plump
clawed feet, exactly hers

and their curious, deathly eyes
she's gloating in bumps
tough as a pair of alligator pumps
all by herself, parthenogenesis

this is not news to science, the cloney sisters
but the news of the day to me
captive and single in a zoo for fourteen years
what a pesky rebel that eight-foot dragon lady
to knock herself up in an afternoon
we won't know for years if the clones
can reproduce themselves, or how much
solitude each dragon girl will need

other scientists report virgin birthings of
male babies who will mate with
their Komodo moms, unstable lineage
I think of Eve and her first sons—
Cain in a jealous rage

Weirdly, scientists call the Komodo ugly
the ugliest species on earth.
Does this sound like science?
Do the green bumps offend
or the indiscriminate fangs?
Who measures ugliness in the
world of hypotheses and evidence?

Who are we to call dragon mama names
so jealous of her uppity powers?
Yet we demur politely regarding
plans to clone destruction, again
our unstable lineage I suppose
descendants of Cain our excuse

a list of recent excuses in my classes

I went to the wrong class
I'm too unemployed to come to class
the doctor says I'm pregnant
but not to get my hopes up
cuz my aunt
has only half her organs
I have a three-week virus
my sister bought me the wrong book
and I couldn't find the campus
I slept too well, too long
I was here on the wrong day
I was here at the wrong time
too sick; didn't want to cough
contagion all over you; did you want me
to cough all over you cause I could
if you want me to
didn't understand the instruction
am too depressed
have a rare case of extreme bi-polar
which makes me more depressed
can't explain the depth of my depression
no babysitter, no car, no gas, no money
no ride no printer no ink or paper no book
don't understand the assignment
I don't want to report on an America poet
I want someone important, an English
poet like Emily Dickinson
I never was good at school

Poem from the Classroom

Today I read your email about
how many of your seven children
are sick and you sick too

I, goddess-like, give you another
three days to turn in your essay
you tell me I am the only teacher
you have met who cares about
her students' education. I think you
must be wrong about this, but wonder
at my colleagues.

Can they not count to seven; did you
not show them the scar from that
fancy surgical birth control? Not likely

Did you not mention birthing three
sets of twins; only one set
where both survived or two sets
where only one survived,
I can't remember. That you had
a tubal ligation but some eggs are
determined survivors?

Did they not
notice that with encouragement
your sentences learn to
begin and end, your evidence gets
commentary and opinions are
supported like children holding hands?

You speak
more languages than I can conceive
and everyone notes that you are

happy. I hope your landlord
fixed your heater; my only help was
to suggest baking potatoes as soon
as you got home, and you turned to me
and said you'd be baking all night:
cakes, bread, everything, smiling at
the thought and at me, as you walked
me to my car because late at night
I have some fear of parking lots.

213 put-downs from the patriarchy mid to late 20th Century or things we got/get called for being female

(inspired by the racial slur "wetback" used Spring 2013 for which the old politician rightfully received a lot of flack)

aggressive, attitudinal, ape-shit, airheads
bitches, babes, bimbos, ball busters, baby-factories, broads
breeders, beavers, bar flies, blondes, busty, bootylicious
boobies, boobs, birds, (old) bags, Baby (cakes), brain dead
concubine, cunts, coozies, courtesans, crazy
commie bitches, chicks, crones, castrating, cock teasers
deficient, ditzy, ding bat, drudges, dusky, doxies
egg heads, effluvia (jk), eager beavers, easy
freeloaders, floozies, freaks, frigid, fatties, flat-chested
& four eyed, firm, fag hag, flake, frumpy, fish wife
glam puss, gold digger, girl, girls, glasses-wearer
gung-ho, gal, gossip, geisha, glamorous
ho, harlots, honey buns, honey, hippy, heavy
hookers & hormonal, honey-pots, homely
harridans, hysterical, histrionic, husband-less, hussy
idiots, ignoramuses, ingrates, ineffectual, immature
jailbait juicey, Jemima, & jelly
kikes kooks, kinky, & kitten
leftie looney, loser, lady, ladies, lax
lazy, loose, lard-ass
man-eating, man-hater, meddling, man-baiting,
matronly, Miss and Missus, minority
money-maker (as in shake your . . .)
nut case, nutcracker, n-words, nymphos, nag, Nervous Nelly
overbearing, ordinary, overweight, old maid, on the rag, old
    hag
princess, prunella, plain-faced, pinko, pussy
plain-jane, priss, pushy, pampered, poon-tang
pussy cat, push-over

queer, queen, quiet, quitter
raging bitch, raging, rabid, Rosy
sugar and slit, skank, skag, squaw, sweetie,
spinster, second-class citizen
tits, town pump, tit-less, thunder thighs, trollop
tease, tootsie, tramp, tomboy, twat
uppity, ugly, useless, underclass
vicious, voracious, voodoo vampires
vixen, va-va-voom, voluptuous
whore, whoring, worthless welfare moochers
the weaker sex, xtra large, y chromosome missing
zit-faced ninny nincompoops

Be Quiet, Please

If necessary, do not speak to those you love
except to listen
if necessary, clip your hair up for air
if necessary, take the blame like custard
on your tongue between less-sweet layers
take the blame like wind
through silky cotton shirts
dare to let him in
if necessary, follow your hunch
trust greased feet to slide you as
pieces fall into place
bus token eyes touch moonlight
quiet as an empty theater seems full
just reach to feel
sand and sea, dust and water
everything touches something.
If necessary, be quiet.

happy 4th of july

noticing today like never, you, limber man set up
like pins for me to roll to, this lifelong romp from when I
in my black slip in my sister's old room, me
trying to be sexy, ridiculous, you didn't laugh at my singing
me, slithering across the room to you
or was it in the grass at my dad's house
or was it when you showed up again
and fixed me vodka tonics or daiquiris
knocked me up, down then up, or was it when we gave up
    smoking
lying cheating and drinking, or cuz you always finish a job
you care about, or maybe because we do call home
I found you and kept you and your manly arms gentle now and
my belly soft and the magic of your silences, your not speaking
if it doesn't help, and it generally doesn't, but sometimes does
    when I insist
and I mean, really insist
or your reluctance to rage, reluctance to seek outside for
    happiness
when you do love what you have and who you are
my gumby man, God, I do appreciate the you-ness of you
I, still, on a tight rope above damnation daily depending on
    aphorisms
to hold us as if we were gravity
as if we balance perfectly

Little Edens

The fires have shown up
bullies spitting at us
we carry our books
lariat thought bubbles
for protection
up and down down and up
removing harm from our lexicons
of shelter and food
even weather doesn't disrupt

we make little Edens out of sand
monuments to perfect days
the whole gestalt
to which we are inclined
no matter what the news
or science says

Arundhati Roy Almost Cried
on Amy Goodman Today

mulling poetic lines over
dead boy friends
like hand-made shrouds
I keep reliving backwards as if
a game boomers play; boomers?
war babies?
having as rumored
more lovers than the average bear
make love not war
layers old Haight Street memories
with nuclear dust
almost time now, almost time
for nuclear dust

frozen global whirling dervish
orbiting us—Pol Pot
walked poets in lines
to killing fields
"nothing is real, and nothing to
get hung about"—
Iraqi poets flee to Paris

moms with her screws loose
peace and poverty hand in hand
war-damaged boyfriend
dads silent on Nam
phrases of Korea muttered
in rainy cold horror jail
we are born again and again
into the state we accept

with a night sky of diamonds
and so much noise to make,
gratitude still the only
working head set

dead exes in my vision like funky
houses on distant hills
Bing Cherries hanging over old
trucks bring sunny summers of
treadle sewing machines
making a living on
simple parts
foot pedal wrought iron
steel wheel sounds of
bottle neck guitar
ribbon shirts & Chairman Mao
peasant blouses Indian
trousers home-made
in America, out of the earth
into the earth
a flesh and blood a
living dream. Arundhati cries
for farmers who are not terrorists

Dear Ms. So and So

Did you just? No, don't call me honey
I'm not honey for your bitches' brew
or a sweetness you yearn for—
don't mistake me innocent of egregious error
don't assume I didn't suffer like
your South Valley years infused with jealousy

This side-kick tough-chick position we were in
a different vehicle in different places, same tools
same disgraces. Fog, rain, ferny redwood forests
had me riding nothing but bitch no matter how
rich, white, or poor, nothing to be jealous of

The colors of women's skin and hair
permeable anywhere to pricks and poisons
booze-soaked fruitcakes
nothing enviable
marriages of madness hurt me too

I never wanted flat formica flavors
perfect linoleum squares, did you?
do you hurl honey at my face
to remind how easily we slide to
the mirror, the replica's terror?

Are we still riding second class mad as hell?
I would flee again out of habit, but flowers
have grown up around me and kindness
these decades the gentlest of handcuffs

The northern states too cold, my dear
too dark, white, too sad
me on a bus with a child
my eyes opened to sun and desert

green chile and bologna sandwiches
sex and Bugler cigarettes
the milk and honey of sage and tortillas
not a given, no picture my parents painted
my mother wept dry rivulets of nonsense
in her golf course reality
my head of honey-colored hair
an extra in their drama

If I was taught to fight
it was a steely back of hand
no slick and steamy switch blade.
My white home silenced—gutted and filleted
me, my sister; Mother girdled us with guilt
a safe I had to blow, oh solitude

Don't call me honey thinking
I'm an imagined platter of plenty
that leaves you hungry
don't call me honey unless to you
I am everything on your table
don't call me honey unless you give
me your bittersweet face in a riotous bouquet
unless you give your own horn of plenty
unless your kiss is husky and thick

Inside out

Old is a silver of us stacked like dolls inside
don't forget the heat, my heart, I tell you, all inside

They say the marriage is painted pretty, a façade
no lips no sound or call, I trip and fall inside

I cry for your gruff full-on touch, warming me hot yet
naming your forgetfulness, I seek a hole to crawl inside

No booze drugs or smoke for respite and flames
it's laughing I yearn for, like dark volcanoes small inside

The children call to see what's for reals, I breathe.
For everyone's troubles, you and I stand tall inside

You buy me an art card your imprimatur de amor
such inking brought me a guffaw inside

Age rolls no icey fog as we make quiet footprints
touch fingers, touch hands, a soft skin thaw inside

The red book says Anything to avoid abandonment
they got that right: our love, lonely love, all inside

Your balding pate under my green eyes, you kiss me, say
Merimee, festoon us lolly garlands, for a festival inside

reunion ambush

heavy like a nine month pregnancy
round like moon basketballs through
hoops

we suffer less with round table
circular beds
houses like teepees, round tents
no sides to take?

the family of falcons down
the street flies linear, celebrating
line drawings for feet
colored spine feathers
soft spotted leopard chests

did I put us in coffins too soon
the sofa my sarcophagus today?
recollecting the family
munching sounds of husband and birds

did I speak too freely too soon
we circled up our wagons
held hands and arms
around the ailing, swatted
the annoying flies of guilt
did I do something unutterable?
utter the un-do-able?

our reunion went swimmingly
the round pool a success
still, worry lurks neglected
don't forsake me
worry calls, like a child's
lips blowing bubbles, like

little boy faces whistling
from the sidelines
I run circles to get away
sleep too much eat too much
and totally forget to pray

I have to kick again and
again here we
go round n round n round

three generations visit the museum

We don't have a steering wheel of chrome chain
no door opening into a yard precisely holding
memories—no grandma saving you with apron love
or relics from splattered
California seeds, our heads, however
above water   unclaimed fruit

no linked family arms for the
Red Rover of us
but the coastal shelf, Sangre de Cristos
El Rio Grande, our brutal life

I have the snap of you tooling down
an adobe path with lunchbox off to school
a happy year where parts fit and time slowed
the fires for morning
a little slice of paradise

the fires of evening restful
for my labor when you were five
and we were just the two of us
at our tiny table
warm tile floors
bright north-facing light
fun until we had no home
when you fell away like handholds dissolving
and I washed out to the sea of us, alone

today with your son, we are three
a blood line marking us
linking us beyond ourselves to
a rich history—we live here
one hour at a time, this museum life
this quiet moment

new rules of love

You came to that first Nar-Anon with me
weighing in on my side; you who lost all siblings
both parents you kept telling me to go.
I'm chairing next month. This is success.

Saturday I drove to Moriarty, no, not named for
Neal Cassidy, but full of drugs, and we laid out brochures.
We talked to mamas who couldn't smile and those who
had learned to smile and cry over the child they are losing,
have lost, might lose to drugs.
We gave some comfort, talking about
Gol Dang, the Gov herself signing for a
a youth facility aqui en Burque—1,000,000 bucks;
addiction, dizzy confusion; smoking seems harmless,
then needles for a fix until breathing ceases.
Two women argued, none of That in our tiny towns.

One old cowboy stopped by about sex offenders; I said wrong
table, but he insisted he could as easily fix them
as fixin' those sheep and pigs he'd been fixin for years.

The pregnancy prevention table had a row
of glaring grandmas looking like cornered rhinos holding
infants, hapless teens in pajama-like clothing,
examples of what happens after unprotected sex.

We had no addicts with us, just pictures
to show: normal, fun-loving kids. We said look,
the young addicts' film shows a roller coaster at Cliff's
Some stop, climb out, walk away. All talk about recovery.
Mothers and grandmas' backbones wobble in place,
spines stacked up like question marks and meltdowns—
A paradox of boundaries and letting go.
Nothing makes sense but all senses involved.

In response to J. Scahill's film "Dirty Wars"
a didactic prose poem

You, Mr. Prez, can order the termination of a person, any
    country on the globe, any given moment you choose. This
    is not front page news.

Hit list 2011 includes an American and his curly-headed son,
    16 yrs old at the mall with friends.
The son searching for his father, the father our special ops
    forces murdered
for speaking out against our, his, US government.

The dear Afghani grandma mourns both son and grandson. The
    camera looks from behind her through the sheer black
    edges of her veil, as if we also were wearing the veil; as if
    we were.

Oh my Republic, the Viet Nam vet mourned years ago. And his
    anguish was palpable, infectious.

In mourning too, the elegant Grandpa no longer has a son to
    see him through. No grandson's joy to revel in, no nada but
    our cowardly assault. Unmanned drones my ass, the
    buttons in Florida and Alamogordo do not push themselves.

We see the boy's face in a video, very clear, perhaps an iPhone
    clip done by a friend.

An American teen laughing in wire-rim glasses, a tall boy with
    a John Lennon laugh, his soft brown curls a Donovan song.
    His tipped-back chin shows, as he laughs, skin
    unblemished, his teeth and jaw, strong.
He would've been a handsome man, jubilant at sixteen.
    Grandma asks the journalist, "What did he do that your
    country killed him, an innocent child?"

Her son an imam born in Las Cruces.

President Obama, your dirty misogynist war drops bombs on
     civilians, leading us into a kiss-ass Kissinger ship, you
     make me Robert McNamara sick, you liar detonating our
     Constitution like tricky Dick, you seem to think if you say
     it then it's legal?

And when they come for you, your women and children,
     perhaps your grandson, or a grand-daughter in utero, will
     that be fair trade?

Fact check NYTimes:

Saturday April 6, 2013 photo

The babies, kids, lined up, tucked in
at the bottom like New Mexico burritos
their faces in repose, shawls loosely covering
child-sized, curly dark heads
They look alive but are quite freshly dead
Living color for war shots unthinkable
but elegant, seven in a row up close
all the frame could contain and still show
roses in their cheeks, well-fed, healthy lips
Their mothers must have died or they would
be bathing with tears and kisses these darlings
wrapped in soft, colored cloths
paisleys, lace, sashes tied like gifts.

And what is the meaning of this word "Sorry"
     one grandfather asks?

Merimée Moffitt arrived in New Mexico in 1970 from Portland, Oregon. She landed in El Rito, then lived in Taos ten years and since then in Albuquerque. She attended UNM to finish her degrees, became a teacher to help pay the bills and had a blessed career. Now retired, she devotes her time to poems, friends, grandkids, and family. She co-hosts ABQ's only open mic prose reading, Duke City DimeStories, which she says keeps her writing.

CPSIA information can be obtained at www.ICGtesting.com
Printed in the USA
BVOW04s1210110916

461797BV00001B/36/P